Wa
around
Helmsley and Ryedale

By

Keven Shevels

Enjoy your walking

Kev Shevels.

TRAIL GUIDES
publications

First published in Great Britain in 2014 by Trailguides Limited.
www.trailguides.co.uk

ISBN 978-1-905444-59-5

The route diagrams in this book are based upon 1925-1940 Ordnance Survey One-Inch maps updated by field trips and site visits.

Trailguides Limited
35 Carmel Road South
Darlington
Co Durham DL3 8DQ

Cover design by Steve Gustard

CONTENTS

Cover photos.
Front. Descending into Riccal Dale. Walk 6 Riccal Dale.
Back cover. Crossing the shoulder of Easterside Hill. Walk 7 The Hills Behind Hawnby.

INTRODUCTION

1. Introduction

Born at Rye Head on the slopes of the Cleveland Hills, the River Rye heads roughly south-east separating the Hambleton Hills to the west and the Tabular Hills to the east before passing Helmsley and leaving the North York Moors National Park. The river cuts a steep-sided valley as it makes it's way down the dale, a valley that presents a wealth of varied countryside for the walker to explore.

As it descends from the Cleveland Hills, the river passes the small village of Hawnby, the largest settlement in the dale above Helmsley. This is a small village, originally settled on a junction of roads and evolving into two distinct halves, the upper village on the side of the hill and the lower part situated next to the river. The village itself is dominated by the two shapely hills of Hawnby and Easterside which rise up behind it and which extend to the moors beyond.

The river continues it's course along the narrow valley passing through both woodland and small fields. This is a rural landscape whose economy has been mainly based on agriculture, although there are occasional glimpses of an industrial past along the sides of the hills.

The Rye then runs to the picture postcard village of Rievaulx, a settlement that grew up surrounding the medieval monastery of the same name. At it's height the monastery itself was one of the richest and most powerful institutions in the north of England. Now all that remains are the spectacular ruins set among wooded parkland.

Continuing it's course, the river then flows past the small market town of Helmsley where it leaves the North York Moors and enters the flat Vale of Pickering. Helmsley is an historic town that grew as a result of it's position at both a road junction and a crossing point of the Rye itself. The centre of the town has retained it's medieval layout around the market place and this has now been designated as a conservation area.

For walkers, Helmsley is noted as being the starting point for the 110 mile (180 km) Cleveland Way. This national trail starts at the main car park for the town and follows a horseshoe loop around the North York Moors National Park before finishing at the coastal town of Filey.

Aside from the Cleveland Way, this small valley and it's surrounding countryside offers a varied backdrop for the walker to explore. A network of footpaths take you along both wooded trails and riverside fields. Above these lie heather-clad moors topped by shapely hills carved from hard Corallian limestone known locally as 'nabs'.

2. Access & the Right to Roam

The land surrounding the River Rye is a mixture of woods, farmland and on the higher slopes and hills above the valley, heather moorland. When walking through most of the lower level farm and woodland, access is generally restricted to public rights of way, in the main footpaths and bridleways. However, once you reach the heather moors access becomes more flexible. The North York Moors are the largest expanse of heather moorland in the country and, as a result, a prime grouse shooting area. In the past access to these moors has been jealously guarded in order to protect the game birds and walkers have been restricted to public rights of way. A policy which has, in many ways, prevented the responsible walker from experiencing some of the best of the moors.

With the implementation of the Countryside Right of Way Act 2000 in 2005 and the introduction of the "Right to Roam" this has changed some of the access rights and certain upland areas of the Moors have now become legally accessible away from public rights of way. This legislation allows walkers the right to roam at will over "designated access land" without the need to be restricted to official footpaths and bridleways.

On the new editions of the Ordnance Survey Explorer maps, this new access land is marked with a light yellow coloured background and at the entry points to this land, the stiles and gates carry the new "access land" waymarking symbol of a brown stick man in a brown circle. The details that accompany each of the walk descriptions will provide information as to whether the route uses rights of way or crosses open access land.

With the right to access has also come responsibility and the walker is expected to observe various limits and restrictions that are placed on their activities at certain times of the year. The landowner and/or farmer has the right to exclude access for up to twenty eight days per year and this is normally applied between May and early July to coincide with the breeding season of the ground-nesting birds on the moors. Where they are known, restrictions that may impinge on any given walk are shown in the details for that walk. However, don't take it for granted that these are going to be accurate as in each year these restrictions may change. Always check any notices that are placed at the access points for any restrictions. To find out more about the `right to roam` and whether any general or specific restrictions apply to any part of the North York Moors then a visit to the website **www.countrysideaccess.gov.uk** will give you all the necessary information.

3. The Walks

The nine walks in this book have all been designed to explore the woods, hills and moors surrounding the town of Helmsley and the valley of Ryedale, while showcasing the landscape and history of this part of the North York Moors. The walks start both from the town itself and also from a number of different locations within and around the valley.

Anybody who has used one of my books before will realise that I have a little bit of a passion for history and how this is reflected in the landscape. As always, this is shown within these walks as I quite frequently use them to visit and explore certain aspects of the countryside that I, personally, find quite interesting. I don't believe that walking guidebooks should be boring and, hopefully, the walks and associated notes will help convey my enthusiasm for the landscape of the North York Moors to you, both as a reader and as a walker.

In the details preceding each of the walks there is an approximate time taken for that particular walk which includes a reasonable time to explore the various sites of interest that are visited. However, this can be variable depending upon how long you, as the walker, take to explore these sites. If you chose not to have a look and investigate then the time taken will obviously be shorter whereas if you linger and have a good mooch about then you may be longer than I have estimated.

The walks in this book have all been graded in accordance with the Ferguson Grading System ('FGS') and the actual grading is set out at the beginning of each individual walk to help you assess their difficulty. A detailed explanation of the FGS and how individual gradings are determined is set out on pages 107-109 in the Appendix to this book.

4. The Weather

Although the North York Moors are not particularly tall in comparison to the Pennines or the Lakeland fells, they are still high, open moorland and as such susceptible to sudden changes in weather. Changes which can present a risk for those walkers who are inadequately prepared.

In summer, when the sun beats down, this open rolling landscape can present very little shade. Therefore, in hot weather you should always carry sufficient fluid or drinks to avoid the risk of dehydration and if prone to the heat or sunburn, wear a hat and/or sunblock.

In contrast, when the weather turns, which it can both surprisingly quickly and with little warning, this same open landscape offers little shelter from both wind and rain. If rain does come, then this is often accompanied by a sudden drop in temperature; even in high summer localised hail and snow are not unknown.

In the autumn and winter months, fog and mist are also a real possibility although the surprising factor here is that it can quite often come from the low-lying Vales of Mowbray and York to the west, creeping along the valleys on the edge of the escarpment and up into the moors beyond.

Looking at a map will show the position of the North York Moors as being adjacent to the North Sea. In most winters this usually makes them one of the first places in the North East to see snow.

Although many of the walks in this book have large sections that remain within the steep-sided valleys that dominate this part of the North York Moors, it is still very important to be properly equipped when venturing out across these low hills and moors.

5. The Maps
Helmsley and the area surrounding it lie on the southern edge of the North York Moors with the valley of Ryedale heading roughly north-west into the heart of the Moors. Only the one map is required for all the walks in this book and that is Ordnance Survey OL 26 North York Moors Western area.

The route descriptions included in this book are meant as a guide and although under normal conditions they should be sufficient to guide you round the route, they are not intended to replace the use of the relevant map. Nor is the sketch diagram of the route meant to replace the OS map but rather to be used as an aid for you to identify the route on this map.

This countryside can be wild and rough, which is part of it's attraction, and the weather can be very changeable. It is quite possible to set off in brilliant sunshine and then to find that later, low cloud and rain has come rolling in and visibility is very poor. The ability to navigate with map and compass is a required skill to safely traverse these hills and it would be extremely foolhardy to venture out with just this guidebook and no map.

6. Facilities, Tourist Information Centres & Websites
Being a small market town and quite a popular tourist destination, the town of Helmsley is quite well catered for in terms of hotels, pubs and cafes and can provide a whole range of accommodation and refreshments. Once you are away from the town, the largest habitation in the upper valley is the village of Hawnby which boasts it's own pub, the Inn@Hawnby, and the Hawnby Tearooms. However, with Ryedale being such a relatively small valley, once you are outside

Helmsley and Hawnby, most settlements are small hamlets or isolated farms although a number of these farms do provide the experience of farmhouse B&B and there is also a number of self-catering cottages throughout the dale. English Heritage also operate a visitor centre at Rievaulx Abbey whose facilities include cafe, shop, toilets and a museum. Further information on accommodation can be obtained from the tourist information centre below or from the visitryedale website.

Within the dale there is the one outdoor shop, Helmsley Outdoors, which, as the name suggests, is situated in Helmsley. Full details are below:
Helmsley Outdoors, 14 Market Place, Helmsley, North Yorkshire, YO62 5BL
Telephone 01439 771628

Unfortunately Helmsley does not have it's own tourist information centre, this service is provided centrally by Ryedale District Council from their centre at Pickering 13.5 miles away, details below. However, the town does have a visitor information point that provides basic information and links to the council's 'visitryedale' website. This is located at the Cut Price Bookstore, 11 Market Place, Helmsley, YO62 5BL.

Pickering Tourist Information Centre.
The Ropery, Pickering
North Yorkshire, YO18 8DY.
Telephone. 01751 473791
Email. pickeringtic@btconnect.com

As well as the visitor centre, Ryedale District Council operate the area's official tourism website at www.visitryedale.co.uk

In addition to the TIC and the official website, there are also a number of other websites that give information on the area in general. Have a look at the following:
www.visithelmsley.co.uk
www.ryedale.co.uk

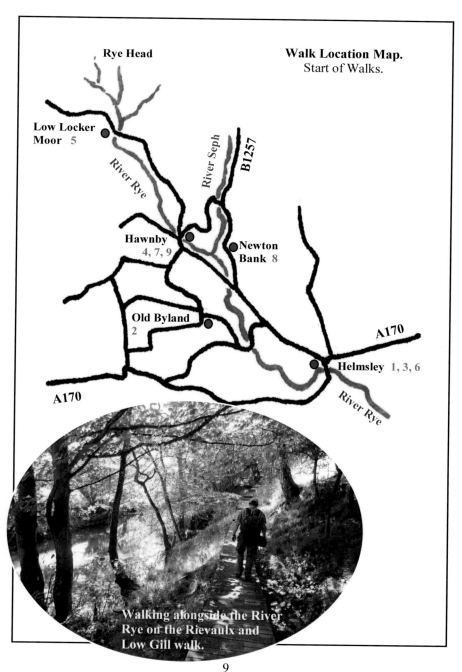

Rye Head

Walk Location Map.
Start of Walks.

Low Locker
Moor 5

River Rye

River Seph

B1257

Hawnby
4, 7, 9

Newton
Bank 8

Old Byland
2

A170

Helmsley 1, 3, 6

A170

River Rye

Walking alongside the River
Rye on the Rievaulx and
Low Gill walk.

The earthworks in the field that are the remains of the medieval grange at Griff. Walk 1: Griff Village Circular.

WALK 1: GRIFF GRANGE CIRCULAR

Rievaulx Abbey is one of the landmarks of Ryedale and at the height of it's power, one of the most important abbeys in the north of England. However, an abbey doesn't exist by religion alone and many of them 'encouraged' gifts of land and property from their benefactors. The patrons of the abbey effectively paying for their salvation. In this way they provided an income upon which the abbey and it's order of brothers could exist but it also enabled the abbeys to become rich and powerful in their own right.

This walk follows the Cleveland Way high above the valley of the River Rye and does a circuit to visit the remains of medieval Griff. One of the monastic granges of Rievaulx Abbey, gifted to the abbey with it's first parcels of land and one of the cornerstones upon which the fantastic wealth of the abbey was based.

DISTANCE: 5.4 miles / 8.7 km.
ASCENT: 659 feet / 201 metres.
TERRAIN: Mainly well-walked path and track along the Cleveland Way with a short section on field path and another short section on road along a quiet, country lane. There are three short, fairly steep climbs but nothing too serious.
START: The entrance to the long stay car park in Helmsley. GR SE 610 838.
TIME: 3 to 3½ hours.
DOGS: Allowed on the public rights of way and also on the permissive paths. However, please keep them on a lead particularly on the permissive paths around Griff Farm. The fields here contain livestock and are used for lambing ewes and young lambs during Spring.
ACCESS: Most of the route is along public rights of way including the Cleveland Way. However, the stretch from Griff Lodge over to the roadside, including the exploration of the field containing the Medieval village, is on permissive footpaths, the permission ending in September 2020.

GRID REFERENCES.

Helmsley car park	610 838
Griff Lodge	591 834
Griff	586 837
Track/road junction	587 846
Road/track junction	580 841
Car park	610 838

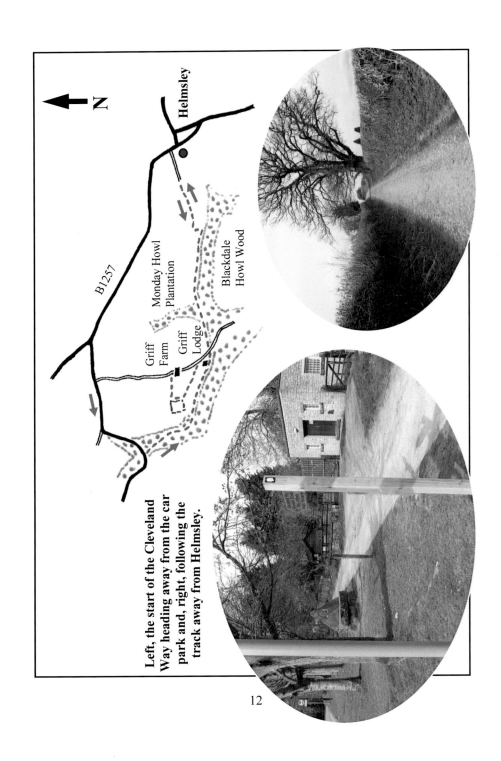

N

Helmsley

B1257

Monday Howl
Plantation

Blackdale
Howl Wood

Griff
Farm

Griff
Lodge

Left, the start of the Cleveland Way heading away from the car park and, right, following the track away from Helmsley.

12

FGS Grading

Grading is T3 [D0, N1, T0, R1, H1]

Distance	0	Up to 6 miles
Navigation	1	Basic navigation skills needed
Terrain	0	75% + on graded track or path
Remoteness	1	Countryside in fairly close proximity to habitation – at least 80% of the route within 2 miles
Height	1	Over 100 ft per mile

THE WALK

1. The Cleveland Way starts it's 109 mile journey to Filey at the entrance to the car park, the start of the walk being marked by a well-signed marker post and a large carved stone.

Cleveland Way
Rievaulx 2½ mls
Filey 109mls
Public Footpath

The start of the Cleveland Way.

As many have done before you, follow the track away from Helmsley. When you come to a turning where the track bears left to Helmsley Walled Gardens, continue straight ahead to a gate and a smaller pedestrian kissing gate that stands next to it.

Go through and follow the well-walked path next to the left-hand fence across two fields. At the end of the second field, go through the kissing gate and turn to the left, following the Cleveland Way sign, and head down to the side of Blackdale Howl Wood.

Here, again following the Cleveland Way marker, follow the obvious path as it turns right to run between the woods on the left and the fields on the right. After a while the path does a little kink to the left to enter Monday Howl Plantation and then descends quite steeply down a flight of stone steps to cross the valley floor before climbing up another flight of steps on the other side.

The steps out of the valley and part of the remains of the army camp.

As you near the top of the climb, you'll notice the remains of old concrete and brickwork, and these continue on when you've reached the top of the bank and go through the lightly wooded area at the top. These are the remains of an old army camp from the Second World War.

Continue following the path through the lightly wooded area at the top of the Howl. It's not long before you come to Griff Lodge where the Cleveland Way crosses a well-made access track. **GR 591 834.**

2. Here, turn right to leave the Cleveland Way and follow the access track past Griff Lodge and through the gateway. A permissive path marker on the right-

Approaching Griff Lodge.

side of the gateway confirms that you are on the correct route.

Follow the track as it bends to the left and then, after a short distance and as it starts to bend to the right, leave it to turn left, following the permissive path marker post, and go through a gateway. Once through, bear right following another marker and go round the edge of the field. As you near the end of the field you'll come to a small pedestrian gate on the right that leads into the field on that side. Go through the gate to enter the field containing the remains of the medieval village of Griff. **GR 586 837.**

3. When you have finished exploring the village leave by heading towards the top corner of the field where the farm lies directly behind it. Go through the waymarked gate and follow the track, with the fence and hedge on your right, towards the farm, passing through a second gate on the way.

You'll come to a junction with a well-made access track just in front of a gate leading into the farm itself. Here turn left to follow the track through a long field to the side of a minor road. **GR 587 846.**

4. Turn left to follow the road as it makes a slow descent. After 500 metres, the road makes a sharp left-hand turn, follow as it makes a steep descent into the valley, known as Ingdale Howl.

As you approach the bottom of the bank and just as the road begins to bend to the right, you'll come to a track on the left-hand side of the road with a Cleveland Way signpost pointing up it. **GR 580 841.**

5. Turn left here to leave the road and follow the track uphill into the woods. The track does a steady climb up the bank and as you get near the top, a line of old quarries lines the left-hand side of the track.

Extending round the side of the bank, these quarries provided some of the limestone blocks used in the building of Rievaulx Abbey.

Continue up the bank and as you get to the top, the track cuts across a second track to go between a couple of waymarked gateposts and then run along the top of the bank, now with open fields on the left. Stay on the track to come back, once again, to Griff Lodge. Here go straight over the access track to retrace your outward steps back along the Cleveland Way to Helmsley, descending and climbing the other side of Monday Howl as you go.

GRIFF GRANGE.

Standing on a level, upland site above the valley of the Rye, Griff was long thought to be the remains of a medieval village that was mentioned in the Domesday Book. However, a survey of the remains by English Heritage in 2002 suggests that rather than being a village they are primarily the remains of a monastic grange associated with Rievaulx Abbey although a medieval vill, or settlement, may have existed on this site prior to the grange.

Part of a wall exposed on the surface of the field.

A grange was the centre of an outlying farming estate belonging to an abbey that provided both food and an income from the sale of produce. Many granges included other associated activities such as mills, quarries and even small metal working sites. These farming estates were not worked by the monks themselves but more often than not by managers and ordinary farm labourers although at times lay-brothers were also involved.

The manor of Griff with four carucates of land was one of a number of estates that were part of the foundation grant made to Rievaulx in 1131. Together with the manor of Stiltons, it formed the grange of Griff which at the time of the dissolution of the abbey in 1538 comprised some 490 acres. Griff being the home grange of the abbey, the home grange being the largest and closest of the abbey granges.

The remains at Griff now lay under pasture with sheep happily grazing amongst the low banks and house platforms. Here and there pieces of the old stone walls can be seen peeping out from beneath the turf. The English Heritage survey and a further one under the North York Moors National Mapping Programme in 2010/11 has identified banks, ditches, field boundaries, a hollow way, fish ponds, buildings, enclosures and evidence of ridge and furrow ploughing. The principal remains comprise of a farmstead which is divided into four parts and which is composed of a number of buildings, some domestic while others are barns. These are surrounded by low earth banks that formed field boundaries and smaller enclosures that were probably used as paddocks. To the west side of the field, a small level platform is thought to have held a chapel that was associated with the grange, after all the monks had to look after the spiritual salvation of those who worked for them.

After Rievaulx was dissolved, agricultural activity continued on the site, there are a number of remains of small farmsteads, yards and paddocks from the post-medieval period to the north of the field. Ultimately, the successors of the grange developed into the modern Griff Farm which lies just to the east.

The name Griff is thought to be of Scandinavian origin as there was a strong Danish influence in the area from the end of the 9th century. The name coming from the Old Norse word 'gryfa' meaning a deep, narrow gully.

The site of the grange is a scheduled ancient monument.

The line of a wall seen as a ridge of different shaded green running across the field.

Rievaulx Abbey. Walk 2: Rievaulx and Low Gill.

RIEVAULX ABBEY.

Framed by the wooded hills that shelter it, Rievaulx Abbey is one of the most impressive sights in the north of England. Founded in 1132 by twelve Cistercian monks from Clairvaux Abbey in France as part of a mission to the north of England and Scotland, it was the first Cistercian abbey in the north. The remote location being ideal for the monks of the Abbey as the Cistercian way of life was to follow a strict regime of prayer and self-sufficiency with as little contact with the outside world as possible.

The remote, wooded valley did not grant the monks all that they wanted however, as a shortage of suitable flat land upon which to build forced them to divert part of the River Rye several metres to the west. In the years following the foundation, the monks altered the course of the river three times in order to acquire suitable land. The technical ingenuity of the monks coupled with an acute business acumen meant that over time, Rievaulx became one of the greatest and wealthiest abbeys in the whole of England. A wealth that was built on the mining of lead and iron and, at a time when English wool dominated the European textile trade, the farming of vast flocks of sheep.

As with many abbeys, the land holdings did not just encompass the abbey buildings themselves but large tracts of land were also owned throughout Yorkshire and other neighbouring counties. In fact the more prominent an abbey became then the more it benefitted from gifts of land from wealthy benefactors seeking salvation. At it's height Rievaulx housed 140 monks with many more lay brothers who were responsible for all the day to day duties and it had also established daughter houses in both England and Scotland. The most important of these being Melrose Abbey which was Scotland's first Cistercian abbey and was endowed by King David.

However, by the end of the 13th century the funding of a number of building projects plus the loss of wool revenue through an epidemic of sheep scab had forced the abbey into a great deal of debt. This situation being further worsened by a number of raids by the Scots in the early years of the 14th century and then by the mid-14th century the influx of the Black Death which decimated the population and consequently the labour force that worked the abbey's farms and granges. By 1381 there were only fourteen monks, three lay brothers and the abbot remaining at Rievaulx although it would slowly recover from this situation.

In 1538, when the abbey was dissolved by Henry VIII, there were said to be 72 buildings with the abbot and twenty-one monks plus one hundred and two servants. The king ordered the buildings to be made uninhabitable and stripped of all valuables such as their lead roofing. As an aside, the dissolution of the monasteries led to such a glut of lead onto the market that the effects were felt on the mining industry for decades. The site of the abbey was then granted to the Earl of Rutland, one of Henry's advisors, until it ultimately passed into the Duncombe family.

The ruins of the abbey are, today, in the care of English Heritage and are open to the public, although there is an admittance fee.

Approaching Rievaulx with the ruins of the Abbey behind the village.

WALK 2: RIEVAULX AND LOW GILL

On the flat topped hills above the Rye valley there are a number of small villages dotted amongst the fields and in many ways these belong to the Rye as the valley itself does. This walk starts from one of these villages, Old Byland, which stands on a broad spur of land high above Ryedale and for a period of time was the home to the second abbey in Ryedale. From the village the walk descends down into Ryedale before passing both the village and the Abbey of Rievaulx. As you walk right past the abbey's front door, so to speak, then it may be worthwhile carrying some money in case you decide to visit this, one of the major religious houses of the north of England during the middle ages.

On the return back to Old Byland, the path passes up the dry valley of Low gill which, on the right day, can itself be a delight to walk. A quiet, secluded valley which gives the impression that the outside world is on a different planet.

Old Byland is an ancient settlement, one of only two in Ryedale that was left standing by William the Conqueror during his Harrying of the North in the years after the Conquest, the other being Helmsley. Tucked away behind the village green lies All Saints Church. Built by the monks of Byland Abbey during the 12th century, while they resided at Tylas, the church replaced an earlier Saxon one. Constructed in the Norman style, parts of the original Saxon building have been incorporated into it, such as the rare semi-circular Saxon sundial in the east wall of the porch, look close to see the ten hours of a Saxon day. As you approach the church, have a look at the winged horses carved into the stones beside the porch, the winged horses being associated with St Oswald, the 7th century Anglo-Saxon king of Northumbria.

DISTANCE: 5.7 miles / 9.1 km.
ASCENT: 564 feet / 172 metres.
TERRAIN: The route is mainly field and woodland paths and tracks although there is a lengthy stretch on quiet country roads as you go through the village of Rievaulx and round Ashberry Hill. There is no significant climbing apart from a short, steep section in the final half mile of the walk as you come back into Old Byland.
START: Old Byland village green, GR SE 550 859. Cars can be parked next to the green but please be considerate to local residents and don't block access.
TIME: 3¼ to 3¾ hours not including any visit that you might make to Rievaulx Abbey.
DOGS: As the route is all on public rights of way, then dogs are allowed. However, be aware that the fields towards the start of the walk normally contain cat-

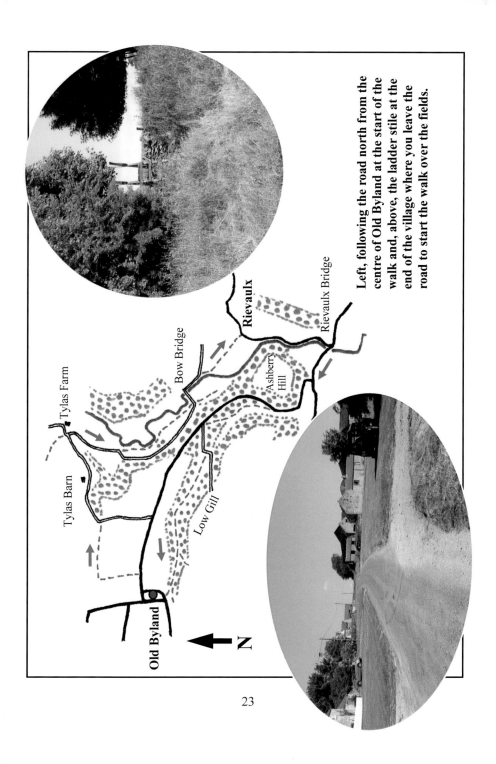

Left, following the road north from the centre of Old Byland at the start of the walk and, above, the ladder stile at the end of the village where you leave the road to start the walk over the fields.

Tylas Farm

Tylas Barn

Bow Bridge

Rievaulx

Rievaulx Bridge

Ashberry Hill

Low Gill

Old Byland

N

tle and at certain times of the year there are young calves with them. There are a number of tall stiles where your dog may need to be lifted over and there is a lengthy road section going through Rievaulx and round to Ashberry.

ACCESS: The route is all on public rights of way.

GRID REFERENCES

Village green	550 859
Path/track junction	557 864
Track/lane junction	565 868
Lane/path junction	564 863
Path/track junction	568 855
Bow Bridge	569 856
Path/road junction	575 851
Road junction	574 843
Road junction	571 844
Road/path junction	568 848
Path junction	567 853
Path/track junction	566 855
Track junction	564 854
Track/path junction	555 857
Path junction	551 857
Village green	550 859

FGS GRADING

Grading is T3 [D0, N1, T1, R1, H0]

Distance	0	Up to 6 miles
Navigation	1	Basic navigation skills needed
Terrain	1	50 – 75% on graded track or path, 25 – 50% off track
Remoteness	1	Countryside in fairly close proximity to habitation – at least 80% of the route within 2 miles
Height	0	Less than 100 ft per mile

THE WALK

1. From the centre of Old Byland, follow the road north to come to a junction. Here turn right to head towards Helmsley and Rievaulx. As you leave the village the last house is on the right side of the road with a small passing place opposite on the left side. At the end of the passing space, partially hidden by a tree, is a footpath marker pointing to a ladder stile that goes over the wall.

Leave the road to turn left and go over the stile and then follow the left side of the field, past the farm buildings, and through a gateway into a second field. Continue to follow the left side and when you get to the end of this second field turn right, so that the fence is still on your left, and walk to a waymarked stile on the opposite side of the field.

Cross the stile and now follow the path as it makes it's way through five fields, staying to the left-hand field edge. At the end of the fifth field, cross the stile with the marker post next to it, on to a track. **GR 557 864.**

Crossing the stile onto the track.

2. You have joined the track next to a crossroads, following the direction of the marker post, go straight ahead down the bridleway to Tylas Farm. The track follows the left side of the steep little valley of Oxendale, high above the woods that line it's sides.

Stay with the track as it goes through a gate before passing to the right of Tylas Barn and then passing through a second gate and starting to descend. The track goes down towards the buildings of Tylas Farm but just before you reach them, comes to a junction with a tarmac lane. **GR 565 868.**

The area around Tylas Farm was the original site of Byland Abbey before it was moved to it's current location near Ampleforth. Fleeing from Scottish raids across the border, the monks left Calder in Cumbria during the 1130's and after a year of wandering were given land near Tylas Farm on which to build a new monastery. However, the close proximity of the already well-established Rievaulx Abbey caused a little bit of distress to the brothers of both abbeys as the bells of each could be clearly heard at both locations. Being the later arrivals in the valley, the monks of Byland gave way and in 1147 moved to Oldstead and then later Byland where the soaring structure that is Byland Abbey was built.

3. Here turn right to follow the lane as it continues the descent into the valley of the River Rye. The lane is followed for around 600 metres until it reaches the valley floor and crosses a small stream. In the height of summer when the vegetation is high you are more likely to hear the stream than see it. Just after you have crossed the stream and before the lane starts to climb again, there is a small path leaving the left side of the road going to a waymarked gate. **GR 564 863.**

The path to the waymarked gate.

4. Leave the road here to go through the gate and follow the green path through the bracken and then across the field. When you get to the other side of the field, the path goes underneath some trees and meets a bend in the River Rye. At this point you also come to a section of duckboards which guide the path along the side of the river.

26

The duckboards bring you to a kissing gate that leads into a field. Go through and the path now descends slightly to run alongside a wire fence. The path passes a marker post before going through a narrow belt of trees and then, ultimately, coming to a gate that leads on to a track. **GR 568 855.**

5. Turn left to follow the track down to the Bow Bridge (**GR 569 856**).

Built in the late 1700's from sandstone blocks, the single spanned Bow Bridge is a Grade 2 Listed Building.

Cross the bridge and follow the track as it turns to the right on the other side. The track slowly starts to climb and then when it begins to bend to the left, you'll come to a footpath marker and a small gate on the right side of the track.

Leave the track to go through the gate and down the steps into the field, then bear left to follow the river downstream. After a short distance you'll come to some trees next to the river and underneath them a kissing gate. Go through the gate and you'll find a marker post with a yellow square on it, this is actually a very faded direction arrow pointing you to the left but you'll have to look very close to tell. Here leave the side of the river to turn left and follow the fence and hedge, keeping them on your left.

The stone for the building of Rievaulx Abbey was quarried locally and the transportation of it was eased somewhat by the construction of two canals on which the stone was ferried by barge. Although now little more than a ditch, the remains of one of the canals can be seen alongside the fence.

The remains of the canal on the other side of the fence.

Follow the fence through a gap into the next field. By now the spectacular remains of Rievaulx Abbey should be appearing between the trees directly ahead. You'll now come to a gate with a small kissing gate alongside it, go through and head directly towards the Abbey, with the hedge still on your left.

When the hedge ends, follow the path as it bears slightly to the right making for a waymarked gate. Pass through and then go straight ahead through a couple of gates to emerge on the roadside in the village of Rievaulx. **GR 575 851.**

Rievaulx is a picturesque little village lying next to the ruins of the abbey from which it takes it's name. While undoubtedly having it's origin as buildings for the abbey complex, most of the cottages in the village have been built with stone that was removed from the abbey ruins.

6. Turn right to follow the road down through the village and past the Abbey. Stay with the road as it runs alongside the river to come, after about 700 metres, to a T-junction. **GR 574 843.**

7. Turn right to cross the river over Rievaulx Bridge and follow the road for a further 400 metres to come to another road junction. **GR 571 844.**

8. Here turn right, heading for Cold Kirby and Old Byland, and follow the road as it goes past the entrance to Ashberry and then bends to the left to go round

More substantial than the smaller Bow Bridge, the three arched Rievaulx Bridge was also built during the 18th century and is also a Grade 2 Listed Building.

the side of Ashberry Hill. After about 400 metres you'll come to a bridleway marker post on the left side of the road, luckily just before the road comes to a steep climb. **GR 568 848.**

9. Turn left to leave the road and follow the path into the trees. The path is well-walked and easy to follow although in places it can be a little bit muddy even during the height of summer. Eventually you'll come to a path junction complete with marker post (**GR 567 853**).

Here bear right to follow the bridleway marker steeply up the side of the hill. After a little bit of a climb, the path emerges on the side of a track, not far from a road a little way over on the right (**GR 566 855**).

Turn left to follow the track back downhill. It is a little bit perverse to head back down straight after climbing steeply uphill but that's public rights of way for you. As you reach the valley floor, the track bends to the left and crosses a very narrow stream. Immediately after crossing the stream, you'll come to a junction with a second track on the right. **GR 564 854.**

10. Turn right here to leave the concrete track and follow the dirt track up the valley. For a while the track is enclosed by the woods on either side and here, in places, it can be quite muddy. Eventually the valley floor emerges into open grassland with the woods now partway up either side of the valley. In summer the track becomes two wheel tracks through the grass, heading up the valley floor.

Leaving the track to continue up the valley floor.

At the top of the valley the track becomes more pronounced and bears left to head steeply uphill (**GR 555 857**) and here leave the track to bear right and follow a faint path as it continues to head up the valley floor.

As the path progresses it becomes clearer and easier to follow and after a short while arrives at a junction (**GR 551 857**).

Here a faint path continues on up the valley but don't follow this. Instead turn right to follow the main path as it makes it's way steeply up the side of the valley. As it nears the top, the path levels out slightly before turning right and emerging next to a house. Go the short distance to the road and then turn right back in to the centre of Old Byland.

Walking through the woods of Beck Dale.
Walk 3: Beck Dale and Ash Dale.

WALK 3: BECK DALE AND ASH DALE

Helmsley is a bustling little market town and for obvious reasons a popular tourist spot. However, not too far away from the town lie two narrow wooded valleys that are really only accessible to the walker and even then they are not visited by too many of them.

DISTANCE: 6.6 miles / 10.5 km.
ASCENT: 499 feet / 152 metres.
TERRAIN: Mainly woodland track and path, although easy to follow the path may be slightly overgrown by ferns and brambles during the height of summer. The two wooded valleys are linked by a section of field paths and a short section of road walking along a quiet lane. There is only the one climb that is not too steep but will make the lungs breath a bit heavily, thankfully it is not too long.
START: The main long-stay car park in the centre of Helmsley. GR SE 610 838.
TIME: 3 to 3½ hours.
DOGS: As the route is all on public rights of way then dogs are allowed. However, you are requested to keep them on a lead especially as you make your way through the pheasant enclosure in Beck Dale.
ACCESS: This route is all on public rights of way.

Grid References

Car park	610 838
Track junction	599 851
Track junction	598 852
Marker post	595 870
Track/path junction	595 872
Path/track junction	593 877
Gate	593 878
Path/road junction	598 876
Road/track junction	599 873
Track junction	603 871
Track/path junction	613 846
Car park	610 838

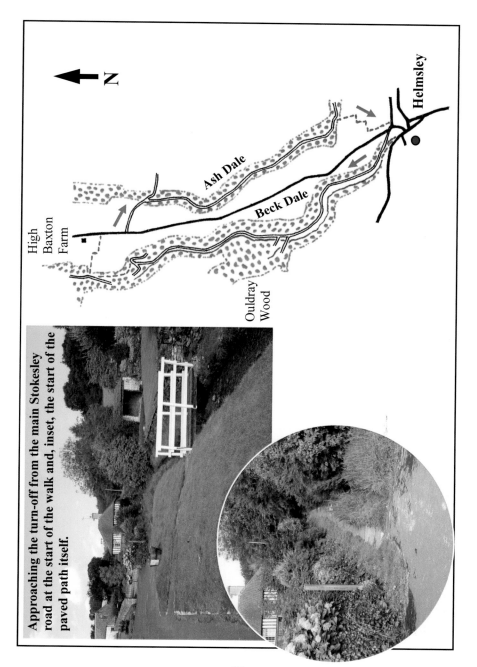

Approaching the turn-off from the main Stokesley road at the start of the walk and, inset, the start of the paved path itself.

N

Helmsley

Ash Dale

Beck Dale

High Baxton Farm

Ouldray Wood

FGS Grading

Grading is T3 [D1, N1, T0, R1, H0]

Distance	1	6 – 12 miles
Navigation	1	Basic navigation skills needed
Terrain	0	75% + on graded track or path
Remoteness	1	Countryside in fairly close proximity to habitation – at least 80% of the route within 2 miles
Height	0	Less than 100 ft per mile

THE WALK

1. Exit the car park, turning right to go back to the main Stokesley road. Once there, turn left to head out of town and take the opportunity to cross the road so that you are on the right-side of it. Go past a turning on the right which is signed as a private road and a short distance later come to a footpath marker post.

Leave the road here to turn right, as indicated by the post, and follow the stone-paved path alongside the Borough Beck for a couple of hundred metres to come to a footbridge. Cross the bridge and follow the path on the other side for a short distance to come to a track and here turn left to follow the track through the woods to a large industrial building that was once a sawmill.

Passing the sawmill.

Stay on the track as it passes to the right of the mill and then runs along the valley floor of Beck Dale with the wooded slopes to the right and a long sheep meadow to the left. Eventually you'll come to a junction with a rough track on the right going off uphill into the trees (**GR 599 851**).

Ignore this turning and continue along the main track on the valley floor. After about 60/70 metres you'll come to a second junction, this one with a footpath marker post. **GR 598 852.**

Approaching the waymarked junction and, inset, pheasants running free in the enclosure.

2. Following the direction of the marker post, turn right to continue following the track along the valley floor passing, after a few metres, a turning on the left that has a small, white 'Private keep out' sign at it's entrance. The track continues along the floor as the valley narrows on either side. After a little while you'll approach a wire enclosure that is built across the track. A waymarked door allows you entrance into what is the largest pheasant enclosure that I've seen. The track makes it's way through the enclosure before eventually passing through a similar gate to exit on the other side.

Once on the other side of the enclosure the valley has narrowed considerably and it has a wilderness feel to it. It's very difficult to imagine that you are not that far away from the tourist centre of Helmsley.

As you walk along the track keep your eye on the skies. Whilst test-walking this route, we saw six hawks circling above the trees, looking for a meal. If you are really lucky you may even catch a glimpse of a deer in the woods.

Continue following the track along the valley floor. After a while you'll pass a rough track on the left, again marked with a small, white 'Private keep out' sign (**GR 599 853**). Not long after this you'll come to a marker post where the track bears right to climb uphill. **GR 595 870.**

The marker post where the track turns right to head uphill.

3. As the footpath marker instructs, stay on the track to go uphill. As you near the top of the bank you'll come to another marker post, this time on the right-side of the track. **GR 595 872.**

4. Opposite the marker post, on the left-side of the track, lies a grassy track that bears left and a path that goes straight up through the conifers. Don't follow the grassy track but instead head up the narrow path through the trees as indicated by the signpost. After a short climb, the path goes over the brow of the hill and then continues along the lightly wooded side of it. The path is easy to follow as it makes it's way along the edge of the valley, even in the height of summer when the ferns are at their highest. After a couple of hundred metres the path arrives at the side of a track. **GR 593 877.**

5. Turn right along the track but only for about 40 metres to come to a small waymarked gate on the right side of the track that leads into a field (**GR 593 878**). Leave the track to go through the gate into the field and then turn left to follow the edge of the field with the fence on your left.

You'll pass through a gateway into a second field and at the bottom of this you'll come to a stile. Cross and immediately turn right along the edge of the field, with the fence on your right, to come to a field corner. Here, following the footpath marker, turn left to continue round the edge of the field, still with the fence on your right, and go through the gate at the end onto a road. **GR 598 876.**

This tarmac road which runs up Baxton's Rigg follows the route of the medieval Magna Via, the Great Road, that ran northwards from Helmsley across the moors. The Magna Via is followed in a later walk, Walk 8 Roppa Edge and the Magna Via, in which more details of this routeway are given.

The track turning off the road, the Magna Via.

6. Turn right to follow the road for about 300 metres until it comes to a slight bend and here you'll find a track leaving the left-side of the road with a footpath marker post pointing down it. **GR 599 873.**

7. Turn left to leave the road and follow the track down towards the treeline, passing through two gateways on the way. Once you are in the trees, the track bends to the right and comes to a junction complete with marker post. **GR 603 871.**

The waymarked junction leading down to Helmsley.

8. Following the direction to Helmsley, turn right to follow the track down the wooded Ash Dale. The track is straight forward to follow as it makes it's way down the valley for almost 3 km with no turnings off. Eventually you'll pass a wooden bench on the right-side of the track and just after that, as the track starts to bear to the left and begin climbing, you'll come to a marker post on the right-side of the track. **GR 613 846.**

The path to Helmsley leaving the side of the track.

9. Leave the track to turn right and follow the path to Helmsley as it goes a short distance through the trees and comes to a small gate leading into a field. Go through the gate and continue straight ahead, following the left-side of the field, to come to a second gate.

Following the side of the field.

Go through this but then immediately turn right to follow the edge of the field, now with the fence on your right, and come to a gate in the field corner. Go through the gate and turn left so that the fence is now on your left and follow it down to the next field corner. Here a waymarker will direct you to turn right and walk alongside the fence, still with it on your left. Ignore the stile in the fence and continue on to the field corner where you will come to yet another gate.

Here turn left through the gate and follow the path alongside the playing field, then along a short enclosed lane and into a small development of bungalows called Warwick Place. Continue straight ahead to the road and then turn right to follow it as it turns to the left to go past the church and arrive onto the main Stokesley road. The entrance to the car park lies just 100 metres to the right on the opposite side of the road.

The trees of Ryedale rising through the morning mist.
Walk 4: The Two Rivers.

WALK 4: THE TWO RIVERS

As it flows through the North York Moors National Park, the River Rye is joined by the River Seph, it's largest tributary while still in the park. The Seph itself flows the length of Bilsdale before joining the Rye at Seph Mouth, a couple of miles east of Hawnby. This walk takes a circular route encompassing the banks of both rivers.

DISTANCE: 4.9 miles / 7.8 km.
ASCENT: 774 feet / 236 metres.
TERRAIN: Most of the route is on field and woodland paths and tracks with a section along a tarmac farm access road. There is a short section of a couple of hundred metres of walking on a public road. Most of the climbing on this walk could be considered as steady although there are one or two small sections that are short and steep.
TIME: 3 to 3½ hours.
START: The car park of Hawnby village hall. GR SE 542 894. The car park lies in the lower portion of Hawnby on the left-hand side of the road to Kepwick, just after passing the Village Store and Tea Rooms.
ACCESS: The route is all on public rights of way.
DOGS: As the route is all on public rights of way then dogs are allowed. However, be aware that a large number of the fields along this route do contain cattle, quite often with young calves, and it may be best not to take your dog with you. .

GRID REFERENCES

Hawnby village hall	542 894
Path/road junction	550 888
Path/track junction	549 886
Track junction	559 877
Track/path junction	559 881
Track/road junction	559 884
Footbridge	562 897
Path/road junction	557 899
Road/path junction	553 896
Footbridge	547 894
Hawnby village hall	542 894

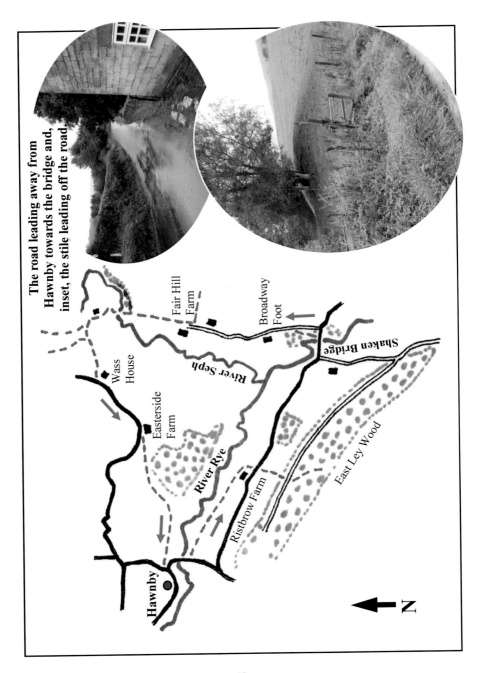

The road leading away from Hawnby towards the bridge and, inset, the stile leading off the road.

Fair Hill Farm

Broadway Foot

Shaken Bridge

River Seph

Wass House

Easterside Farm

River Rye

East Ley Wood

Risibrow Farm

Hawnby

N

FGS GRADING

Grading is T5 [D0, N1, T1, R1, H2]

Distance	0	Up to 6 miles
Navigation	1	Basic navigation skills needed
Terrain	1	50 – 75% on graded track or path, 25 – 50% off track
Remoteness	1	Countryside in fairly close proximity to habitation – at least 80% of the route within 2 miles
Height	2	Over 125 ft per mile

THE WALK

1. Exit the car park and turn right to go past the village shop and tea rooms to the road junction. Here turn right to follow the road to Helmsley and cross the young River Rye via Hawnby Bridge.

Hawnby Bridge.

Once on the other side of the bridge, you'll come to a footpath marker post and a stile on the left-hand side of the road.

Cross the stile but don't follow the side of the river. Instead go up the bank on the right and then go across the field to a visible gate and stile on the other side.

Cross the stile and, ignoring the path created by the livestock, go straight across the field to a waymarked stile that lies a little bit down, on the left, of the gate on the opposite side.

Again go over the stile and go straight ahead crossing the slope of the field. Along the way you'll pass a footpath marker post, to the left of a group of trees, which will guide you to a waymarked gate and stile. The buildings of Ristbrow Farm sit to the right on the bank above you.

Cross the stile and, following the direction of the waymarker, turn right to head up the bank to a gate and waymarked stile that leads onto the side of a road. **GR 550 888.**

2. Cross the road to the footpath marker and stile on the opposite side and go over the stile into the field. Go straight ahead up the bank making for the line of trees above you. At first it's very difficult to see but as you get closer you'll find a waymarked stile hidden under the trees.

Heading towards the waymarked stile under the trees.

Cross the stile and then bear right to follow the path through the bushes to a marker post. Here the path now turns to the left to go quite steeply up a short bank and arrive at the side of a track. **GR 549 886.**

3. Turn left onto the track and, ignoring the path on the other side of the track, follow the track for the next 1½ km as it makes it's way through East Ley Wood. Eventually you'll come to a gate across the track, go through to come to a waymarked track junction. **GR 559 877.**

East Ley Wood and, inset, the marker post at the side of the track.

4. Turn left to follow the track downhill passing through a gateway along the way. After a little while you'll come to a large marker post on the right side of the track (**GR 559 881**).

Here leave the track and turn right, following the direction of the post to Shaken Bridge, and go down the bank to a wooden fence and gate. Pass through the gate and go up the little bank on the other side to come to a farm track. Turn right to follow the track downhill and come to the side of a road. **GR 559 884.**

5. Turn right onto the road and follow it the short distance to cross Shaken Bridge that spans the River Rye. Follow the road a short distance up the bank on the other side to come to a bridleway marker post and small gate on the left side of the road.

Here, turn left to leave the road and go through the gate and enter the wood. Follow the path up through the wood, passing through a second gate, and arriving at the side of a concrete track.

Turn left to follow the track uphill. After a little while you'll come to the buildings of Broadway Foot which stand on the left of the track, most of the buildings appear to be in ruins. Here a bridleway comes in on the right of the track but ignore this to continue along the track, which has now changed it's surface to tarmac, following the small sign which points straight ahead to Fair Hill Farm.

Following the track to Fair Hill Farm.

Continue along the track and after a little while you'll pass the entrance to a farm and here follow the bridleway sign to stay on the track as it bends to the left.

It's not long now before you approach the buildings of Fair Hill Farm. As you get level with the first building, turn right to leave the track and go up to the footpath waymarker post next to the fence. Ignore the bridleway marker on the right and cross the stile that has two footpath markers on, to enter the field.

Once into the field, turn left to follow the left-hand fence. The fence starts to descend and here you'll come to a gateway in it. Go through the gateway so that the fence is now on your right-side and you'll come to a broken marker post. Now go straight ahead to a second gateway that is a short distance in front, there is a waymarker on the left-hand gatepost next to the broken stile.

Pass through the gateway and go across the next field but bearing slightly to the left, going down the slope of the hill. Make for the end of a line of bushes and trees and when you get there, ignore the path that goes into them and continue downhill to a visible footbridge across the River Seph. **GR 562 897.**

The footbridge across the Seph.

46

6. Cross the bridge and once on the other side continue straight ahead to join a green track that comes down the hill in front. Turn right to follow the track uphill where it disappears once you have reached the top of the edge of the valley.

Here there is a fence in front of you but turn left to make for the stone barns on that side. When you get to them, go through the gateway on the left of the barns and follow the track that leads past them. Once past, stay on the track as it bears left and after a short distance come to a three-armed footpath marker post.

Turn left here to leave the track and follow the grass path uphill to a gateway. Go through and follow the left-hand fence until you come to where the ground slopes steeply down into some woods. Here bear right to follow the edge of the slope round to come to a footpath marker post.

Follow the direction of the post and turn right to go up the bank to a way-marked stile. Cross and bear left to a second stile. Cross this and go ahead but bearing slightly to the right, staying above the slope, to come to a third stile which leads you onto the side of a road. **GR 557 899.**

7. Turn left to follow the road, going past the entrance to Wass House. After 500 metres you'll come to Easterside Farm and just past this farm, on the left-hand side of the road, you'll come to a gate and footpath marker post. **GR 553 896.**

The gate and marker post at the side of the road.

8. Turn left to leave the road and go through the gate into the field. The direction shown by the footpath marker is slightly out so don't blindly follow it. Instead head diagonally down across the field to the left of the first electricity pole, to the bottom fence of the field where you will find a gate and stile underneath the overhanging trees.

Cross the stile into the wood and then follow the path through the narrow belt of trees. Once past these, the path enters a small field and here turns to the left to go down to a gate. Go through the gate to enter a long open field and now follow the path as it heads down the length of the field.

As you get towards the bottom of the field you'll have to cross the line of an obvious ditch, the bottom of which is a little soft and muddy. After this, turn right to the edge of the field to find a waymarked stile and footbridge hidden in the trees. **GR 547 894.** If you miss the ditch and continue down the field then you'll come to a fence and gate, in which case you'll know that you have come too far and you'll need to retrace your steps.

9. Cross the stile and footbridge and follow the path across the next field to a waymarked gate. Go through and the buildings of Hawnby can be seen directly in front, follow the path as it heads directly towards them to come to a gate that leads onto the road at the road junction in the lower half of the village.

Heading towards the buildings of Hawnby.

Cross the road and head up the side road, passing the Hawnby Stores and Tea Rooms, to come back to the village hall and it's car park.

Passing along the edge of Scugdale.
Walk 5: A Circuit of Rye Head.

WALK 5: A CIRCUIT OF RYE HEAD

The Rye flows through the gentle, rolling Hambleton Hills down to Helmsley and then enter the Vale of Pickering. However, it begins life on the harsher Cleveland Hills further to the north. This route is a high moorland walk that encircles Rye Head, the shallow moorland bowl that acts as the gathering ground for the springs that join to form the infant River Rye. Along the way the walk passes a number of sites that date back to the prehistoric Bronze Age, over four thousand years ago when the climate was much milder and these hilltops were prime agricultural land supporting a sizeable population.

DISTANCE: 9.3 mile / 14.8 km
ASCENT: 974 feet / 297 metres
TERRAIN: Most of the route is on well-made moorland tracks, however, the final stretch from Dale Head back to the parking space is across moorland path which is normally quite wet and muddy. There are no strenuous climbs along the route, more long and steady.
TIME: 3¾ to 4¼ hours.
START: Car parking space at Low Locker Moor on the Osmotherley to Hawn-by road. GR SE 511 944.
DOGS: Not allowed on the open access land.
ACCESS: The route is a mixture of public rights of way and tracks over open access land.

GRID REFERENCES

Parking space	511 944
Farm yard	517 953
Track junction	524 963
Track junction	531 969
Track junction	532 977
Track junction	528 981
Track junction	527 982
Track junction	517 990
Track/path junction	506 989
Track junction	496 981
Track junction	494 978
Track junction	492 972
Faber's Stone	491 970

Above, the road leading uphill away from the parking space and, below, the track leaving the road at Low Cote Farm.

Scugdale

Arnsgill Ridge

Hillend Farm

Low Cote Farm

River Rye

Parking Space

Locker Low Moor

Pin Howe

Rye Head

Whorlton Moor

Swainby Shooting House

Dale Head

Miley Pike

N

Track/road junction	490 955
Road/track junction	488 955
Bridge	497 947
Gate	507 944
Parking space	511 944

FGS GRADING
Grading is F4 [D1, N1, T0, R1, H1]

Distance	1	6 – 12 miles
Navigation	1	Basic navigation skills needed
Terrain	0	75% + on graded track or path
Remoteness	1	Countryside in fairly close proximity to habitation – at least 80% of the route within 2 miles
Height	1	Over 100 ft per mile

THE WALK

1. From the parking space turn left to follow the road uphill until you come to Low Cote Farm. Here the road bends sharply to the left but a track continues straight on passing in front of the farm buildings. There is a bridleway sign 'to Chop Gate' on the corner of the wall on the left, hidden by the bushes.

Leave the road to follow the track as it starts to head back down to the side of the young River Rye. As you reach the valley bottom, ignore the bridleway that goes off on the right and crosses the river, and continue straight ahead.

In front the young Rye bends to the left while it's tributary, Arns Gill, cascades over a small waterfall before joining the river.

The track now crosses a bridge over the Rye and once across starts to climb. At the top of the bank you'll come to a junction and here, following the bridleway to Chop Gate, turn right towards Hill End Farm and after a little distance enter it's yard. **GR 517 953.**

2. In the yard, just before you actually get to the buildings, you'll come to a marker board in front of you with a couple of yellow markers on. Here turn left to go through the gate with a blue and white bridleway marker on it that lies a short distance away. The track now goes uphill to cross a short field to another gate.

To the left of the gate the remains of an old lime kiln can be seen. In years past nearly every farm on the moors had either it's own small lime kiln or access to one. Within the kiln, layers of wood and limestone would be placed with the resulting blaze reducing the limestone to powdered lime. This would then be spread over the fields as a fertilizer to "sweeten" the grass. This agricultural practice is responsible for the characteristic moorland landscape of open moor next to green grassed grazing fields. Many lime kilns date back to the 1700/1800's, however, their use ended when an alternative, cheaper method of chemical manufacture was developed.

Pass through the gate and continue on to a second gate that opens onto the open moor. Continue to follow the main track and after a short distance you'll pass, on the left, the small quarry that was the source of the limestone used in the kiln.

Over on the right you'll have no problem identifying the tall, slender shape of the Bilsdale transmitter mast rising high into the sky. The sight of the mast is a permanent feature throughout much of this walk. The track continues above a small wood over on the right and as you pass, two minor tracks head away down to it, both of which you ignore to continue on the obvious main route. Eventually you'll come to a track junction. **GR 524 963.**

3. Ignore the turning on the right and continue following the main track straight on along the side of Arnsgill Ridge. After a while you'll pass a line of grouse butts with their white-tipped marker posts and a rough access track going off both sides of the main track. Continue on and you'll shortly come to another track junction. **GR 531 969**.

4. Here turn left to start climbing slowly uphill once again. After a while you'll pass a faint track on the left which goes off to some grouse butts but continue straight on along the main track to come to another junction, again with a track on the left. **GR 532 977.**

5. Turn left to follow this track. After a long while you'll eventually pass a rough track on the left (**GR 528 981**) and not long after you'll pass through a line of grouse butts before arriving at a junction with a track on the right. **GR 527 982.**

6. Here, turn right and the track starts to climb slightly, passing an old boundary stone on the right that is covered with a large branch of an old tree giving it a strangely distorted shape especially if the mist is down (**GR 527 983**).

The old boundary stone.

Continue on the track as it now goes over the top of the ridge and as it starts to descend, bears to the left to go along the edge of Black Moor, high above the Scugdale valley.

Roseberry Topping framed in the gap between the hills and, inset, approaching Scugdale.

As you approach the side of Scugdale, you are presented with a brilliant view out over the escarpment to the north. The first gap between the hills frames the cone of Roseberry Topping standing isolated from the main escarpment over in the distance. The second gap between the hills presents a not quite so scenic view, the Teesside chemical industry situated in the far distance next to the river.

Eventually the track comes to a junction with a second track on the left. **GR 517 990.**

7. Continue straight ahead as the track starts to descend into a dip as it heads along the edge of Scugdale. As it starts to rise again, the track bears to the left to move away from the side of the valley and go over the shoulder of Coal Hill.

As you come to the high spot of the shoulder, a faint path leaves the right-side of the track to go across the heather to the summit of the hill. **GR 506 989.** It's only a short walk to visit the Bronze Age burial mound of Pin Howe, located on the top of the hill.

Standing on the edge of the hills overlooking Scugdale, Pin Howe is a very prominent position and over 4,000 years ago this prominence led to the siting of a round barrow on it's summit. Standing 0.75 metres high and 10 metres in diameter, this stone and earth mound is now much reduced compared to when it

Pin Howe.

was originally constructed but when it was new, it must have been highly visible throughout the surrounding area.. As part of their architecture, round barrows are normally surrounded by a ditch but time and erosion have conspired to fill this in and it is no longer traceable on the ground. Conversely, unlike most barrows on the North York Moors that have been excavated, the one on Pin Howe has the appearance of being undisturbed.

8. Continue on the track as it now bears left and starts to descend. After a little while you'll pass a rough track on the left and then a little bit later another one on the right. However, stay on the obvious main track as it heads towards a stone -built shooting hut that you can see a short way in front. Just before you get to the hut, you'll come to a junction with a track on the right. **GR 496 981.**

On the left of the track is Swainby Shooting House. Built during the 1800's this stone building provided the base for a day's shooting for the Victorian sportsman. Between drives, where the grouse were driven towards the guns by beaters, they would retire to the house for refreshments provided by the staff brought up from the lodge. The house is more functional than ornate, plain stone walls and no windows. It was not designed for habitation and no windows made it more weatherproof.

On the opposite side of the track to the shooting house stands the Nelson Stone. Dating back to around 1200, the stone is one of a number of old stones marking the boundaries of Whorlton, Osmotherley and Snilesworth. The name Nelson

Swainby Shooting House and the Nelson Stone.

derives from Nelehou. For many years a Victorian stone, similar in carving to the one at Faber's Stone, stood next to the Nelson Stone but seems now to have disappeared.

9. Continue straight ahead to the hut, Swainby Shooting House, where the track bends to the left and continues across the moor curving round the top of Rye Head. The birth place of the River Rye.

After a couple of hundred metres, you'll come to a junction with a track on the right where an old boundary stone stands at the junction (**GR 494 978**).

Standing at the junction is another old boundary stone, this one being marked with an OS benchmark. A benchmark is an aid to the mapmaker and is cut into rock or stone, normally on churches or bridges. Things that are unlikely to be pulled down so it is quite unusual to see one on a boundary stone. The mark is a wedge-like horizontal notch above a broad arrow. The arrow being the sign of the War Department who originally controlled the Ordinance Survey. The mark indicates an ascertained height or level and when a Surveyor is "levelling" he would fit an angle iron into the notch as a bench or support for his levelling staff and would then work from this known benchmark.

Continue straight ahead as the track slowly climbs up a gentle rise to come to another junction, this time with a track on the left. **GR 492 972.**

10. Continue straight ahead as the track climbs up the ridge. When you get to the top of the rise, the double boundary stone of Faber's Stone stands a short distance to the right of the track. **GR 491 970**.

Standing next to the track are two stones known collectively as Faber's Stone, both marking the estate boundary as it runs along the ridge. The older stone has possibly been here since the 1200's, it is in similar condition to the Nelson Stone which was encountered a little earlier along the same boundary and which is known to have been in place since that date. The younger, more ornate stone has been in place since the 1800's, have a close look at the markings, they are a fine example of the stonemason's craft. This and other similar stones will have been erected during the heyday of Victorian grouse shooting, newer, more ornate stones replacing the old, plainer ones. A sign of wealth, power and influence and even possibly just showing off to the invited guests of the shooting parties as they made their way past to the butts.

Continue on the track as it now starts to descend before climbing up another rise named Miley Pike.

The track bends to go to the left of the summit. The summit top and the prehistoric burial mound that sits on it are easily accessible across the heather.

Miley Pike tumulus is a scheduled ancient monument and is another example of a Bronze Age burial mound located on the top of a prominent landmark, probably acting as the dual purpose territory marker. However, you'll notice that many of the stones that make up the summit have been shaped and smoothed off, not at all like the natural stone used on these mounds. Long before it was declared a monument, the Victorian landowner built a stone shooting house on the summit of this hill. Now the top is a combination of the natural stone of the tumulus and the carved stone walls of the house.

The track now descends and after a few twists and turns finally reaches the side of a road. **GR 490 955.**

11. Turn right to follow the road for a couple of hundred metres to come to a track entrance and bridleway sign on the left-side of the road. **GR 488 955.**

12. Turn left here to leave the road and follow the track down to a gate. Go through and follow the track as it bends to the left to go down the small valley. After a while and as you approach a gate in front of the ruined buildings of Dale Head, you'll pass the remains of an old lime kiln over on your right.

Go through the gate and follow the track as it goes between the buildings and then, at a marker post, turns left to go down the short bank to a waymarked gate.

Pass through the gate and then turn right to follow the fence on the right, passing a marker post on the way, as you head down to a large wooden bridge. **GR 497 947.**

13. Cross the bridge and follow the path up the bank on the other side as it goes up onto Low Locker Moor. The path now goes across the side of the moor and as it does passes through a prehistoric field system.

Once on the other side of the moor, the path comes to a gate in a wall. **GR 507 944.**

14. Pass through the gate and follow the hollow way that runs next to the wall on the right. Continue past a gate in the right-hand wall and then when you get to the bottom of the field you'll come to another gate. Go through onto a track and here, turn left to follow it down the bank to another gate, a bridge over the beck and then your car.

LOW LOCKER MOOR SETTLEMENT

Four thousand years ago the climate on the North York Moors was warmer and more favourable than it is today. What we now see as heather moorland was light woodland consisting of ash, elm and hazel. During this period, known as the Bronze Age, human settlement across these hills was quite extensive, the Moors supporting a higher population density than they do now. At this point the population had moved from a hunter/gatherer to a more settled farming style of life, settling in small communities of extended families in homes that were cleared from the woodland.

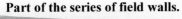

Part of the series of field walls.

The settlement and field system at Low Locker Moor is one of these communities consisting of a series of fields, stone clearance cairns, two round barrows and a large hut circle. The hut circle is located on the left side of the path, on the level space close to the side of the Wheat Beck and is surrounded by a number of low stone walls that form small enclosures, possibly gardens or animal pens. The hut circle is 13 metres in diameter and is comprised of a ring of stones that would have formed the foundations of a round house, a style of housing that was both practical and popular and whose usage spanned several thousand years from the late prehistoric to well within the Roman age and beyond. At 13 metres (43 feet) the round house would have provided ample accommodation for a reasonably sized family group.

Further up the side of the hill there are a series of tumbled stone walls, on both sides of the path, that run at right-angles to the beck, some for a distance of up to 400 metres. Between these parallel lines of walls, there are a number of cross-walls that help form a series of small, rectangular fields. The whole being part of an early cultivation system. Within the fields are seventeen irregular mounds of stone which vary in diameter and can be up to 0.5 metres in height. These are clearance cairns, formed as stones were thrown to one side as the field was cleared for planting.

The remains of the hut circle.

As part of the field complex, there are also two round barrows, several hundred metres apart and quite distinctive from the clearance cairns. These are burial sites for the inhabitants of the settlement. They have long since been robbed out so it is unknown whether they contained the remains of one individual or whether they were a communal grave.

The layout of the fields is symmetrical with that of another field system that lies on the opposite bank of the Wheat Beck.

One of the two round barrows.

Following the track along the
floor of Riccal Dale.
Walk 6: Riccal Dale.

WALK 6: RICCAL DALE

The River Riccal lies a short distance away from Helmsley and is a tributary of the River Rye, joining it a few miles south-east of the town. The river is formed by the meeting of two streams coming down from the moors before it starts a slow meandering course through a narrow valley cut into the Tabular Hills. This slow meandering is what has given the river it's name, in the 14th century it was known as Ricolvegraines meaning Rye Calf where the word Calf is a small island near a larger one. The islands being formed by the changing course of the meandering river.

The river valley is, as one look at the map will show, one long woodland. Unlike many of the more modern plantations comprised mainly of conifers, the valley is mainly the more native broadleaved trees being wooded with hazel, birch and especially beech. In spring the ground is covered by large groups of bluebells giving vast swathes of colour. However, even in autumn when the leaves are differing shades of colour, this wooded valley is a joy to walk.

DISTANCE: 7.2 miles / 11.5 km
ASCENT: 551 feet / 168 metres
START: Helmsley main car park. GR SE 610 838.
TERRAIN: Mainly field and woodland paths and tracks. The descent into and the climb out of Riccal Dale are fairly steep but are not particularly long and so not too bad.
TIME: 3½ to 4 hours.
ACCESS: The route is all on public rights of way.
DOGS: As the route is on rights of way then they are allowed. However, if your dog is one that chases birds then you may have trouble controlling them as the woods are full of pheasants strolling around. This also means that during the shooting season your dog may hear a few loud bangs. Livestock will also be encountered as you cross the fields in the early and finishing stages of the walk. There is also the probability that you will meet the farm dogs as you cross the yard at Reagarth Farm.

GRID REFERENCES

Car park	610 838
Gate	630 847
Path/track junction	626 852
Gateway into woods	621 866

Heading up the lane at the start of the walk.

Rea Garth Farm

River Riccal

Reagarth Farm

A170

Helmsley

N

Track junction	619 872
Path/track junction	621 874
Track junction	622 875
Track junction	621 870
Track junction	622 868
Track junction	622 867
Track junction	622 864
Track crossroads	627 856
Track/path junction	632 846
Gate	630 847
Car park	610 838

FGS Grading

Grading is T4 [D1, N1, T1, R1, H0]

Distance	1	6 – 12 miles
Navigation	1	Basic navigation skills needed
Terrain	1	50 – 75% on graded track or path, 25 – 50% off track
Remoteness	1	Countryside in fairly close proximity to habitation – at least 80% of the route within 2 miles
Height	0	Less than 100 ft per mile

THE WALK

1. From the car park, exit onto the B1257 Stokesley road and turn right to head into town, taking the opportunity to cross and walk on the left-hand side of the road alongside All Saints Church. When you come to the road junction, turn left to go past the entrance to the church and follow the road past the market place, heading out of town towards Scarborough.

As you reach the outskirts of the town, you'll come to a road on the left, sign-posted to Carlton and Bransdale, opposite the garage on the right-side of the road. Here turn left and follow the right-side of this side-road for 100 metres until you come to a footpath marker post pointing down a lane between the houses.

Turn right to go up the lane and when you come to the end of the tarmac, continue across the grass to the waymarked left-hand gate. Go through the gate into the field and head diagonally down the length of it towards a couple of white notice boards on the left-hand side. Once there follow the fence on the left to a waymarked gate.

Heading across the field to the left-hand fence.

Go through the gate and follow the right-hand edge of the field as it goes round, passing a gateway and some more notice boards, before eventually arriving at another waymarked gate, this one being next to an electricity post. Once through the gate, continue straight ahead, with the hedge on your right, past the bottom of Monk Holme Wood to another waymarked gate.

Pass through and, following the direction of the waymarker, bear left past the end of the wood and over the rise where once you are at the top, the buildings of Reagarth Farm come into view. Head to the right of the large barns, passing a fence corner, and you will come to another waymarked gate.

Go through the gate to cross the yard to the waymarked left-hand gate opposite and once through this and into the next field, follow the hedge on the right towards the line of trees that mark the top of Riccal Dale Woods. As you follow the hedge you'll go past a gateway on your right and at the bottom of the field you'll come to an unmarked gate in the field corner that leads into the woods. **GR 630 847.**

2. Go through the gate and follow the path into the trees. Within a few metres you'll come to a path junction with yet another of the notice boards stood next to it. Ignore the path on the right that heads downhill and follow the path that bears left and runs just inside the top of the wood.

This path is followed for around 800 metres with the fields a short distance way on the left and the slope down into Riccal Dale on the right. Eventually you'll pass what seems to be a graveyard for old farm machinery and shortly after you'll exit the trees and come to the side of a well-made vehicle track. **GR 626 852.**

3. Turn right to follow the track and after 50 metres come to a junction with yet another notice board next to it. Here ignore the right-hand branch that goes downhill and continue straight ahead past an old piece of machinery.

This rather substantial piece of metalwork appears to be some sort of crusher and may be related to the small quarry that lies just over the lip of the hill next to it.

Continue along the track as it runs along the outside of the wood making for Rea Garth Farm (notice the subtle difference in spelling between this and the last Reagarth Farm). As you approach the farm, you may notice a waymarked stile on the right going off into the woods, ignore this and continue on the track as it goes between the buildings of the farm and into the fields behind.

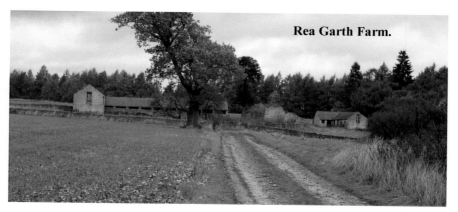

Rea Garth Farm.

Stay on the obvious main track as it goes between the woods on the right and the fields on the left and ignore any minor side tracks that leave it. Eventually the track passes through a gateway to enter the woods. **GR 621 866.**

4. Stay on the track as it goes into the woods, still staying above the valley on the right. After a few metres pass another track on the right that goes down into the valley and continue straight ahead as the track starts to slowly climb.

You'll pass a further two minor tracks on the left before the track comes to the top of the ridge and here it turns sharply left and a grass track continues straight on. **GR 619 872.**

The path heading right, downhill from the junction.

5. Here at the bend, leave the main track but also ignore the grass track that goes straight ahead. Instead turn right to find a substantial path that descends down into the valley. Soon after starting on it, the path bears to the left to descend gradually down across the slope of the hill.

Initially the path is fairly easy to follow but as you get further down the line of the path does become harder to trace but only for about 100 metres or so. Resist the urge to head straight down the slope to the narrow track that you should be able to see below you and continue down across the slope of the hill and the path will re-emerge and will then, in a short distance, join the narrow track below you. **GR 621 874.**

6. Turn left onto the narrow track and follow it as it continues the descent into the valley. After around 200 metres it will come to a junction with some more substantial vehicle tracks on the valley floor. **GR 622 875.**

7. Turn right to follow the vehicle track which then starts to climb a small rise and when you get to the top, you'll meet a junction with a track on the right (**GR 621 870**). Ignore the right-hand track and bear left to descend down to meet another junction, this time with a track on the left which goes past a large wooden shooting hut (**GR 622 868**).

Continue straight ahead and after a 100 metres you'll come to another junction of tracks (**GR 622 867**). Here follow the blue waymarker and bear right to start a slight climb before, after a short while, starting to descend back down again and passing a track that goes off to the right (**GR 622 864**). Eventually the track comes down to the side of the River Riccal and meets a footpath sign on the left of the track (**GR 624 861**).

Ignore the footpath and continue along the track as it makes it's way up a slight rise and moves away from the river. As it goes round a bend, ignore the footpath marker on the right (**GR 627 859**) and continue on the track to come to a cross roads. **GR 627 856.**

8. Here leave the main track, which bears right to go uphill, and follow the waymarker straight ahead along the minor track. Continue along the valley floor, passing a small footpath

Approaching the crossroads.

marker post on the left, and after a little while you'll pass another marker post again on the left of the track (**GR 628 853**).

The track now starts to climb away from the river before descending again but not going all the way back down to the water and coming to another waymarker post, again on the left of the track (**GR 632 847**). Ignore the marker post and continue on the track as it goes a short distance round a bend and comes to yet another marker post but this time on the right side of the track. **GR 632 846.**

9. Leave the track at this marker post and turn right to follow a well-walked path as it makes it's way up through the trees. As you get to the top of the bank, you'll come to a path junction marked by a notice board. This point may seem familiar to you as you passed here on the outward leg of this walk. Follow the path left for a few metres to the gate that leads out of the woods and into the field. **GR 630 847.**

The path leaving the track and heading uphill through the woods.

10. From this point you are retracing your outward steps back to Helmsley. So go through the gate and follow the left-hand hedge across the field to come to the waymarked gate leading into the yard of Reagarth Farm. Head straight across the yard to the waymarked gate on the opposite side and once through and into the field, head downhill making for the left of the wood to come to another waymarked gate.

Once through this, follow the left-hand hedge straight ahead, ignoring the sheep trod that bears right, to the next gate. When you have gone through this, bear left to follow the edge of the field round to come to another waymarked gate.

Go through and follow the path alongside the right-hand fence till you come to the notice boards. From here bear diagonally across the field to the gate in the left-hand corner of the field. Once through the gate, follow the lane straight ahead to the road and then turn left to come to the main Scarborough road.

Now it's a case of turning right and following the road back into the town, past the market place and when you get to the road junction next to the church, turning right to come to the car park entrance.

Looking back at Hawnby Hill.
Walk 7: The Hills Behind Hawnby.

WALK 7: THE HILLS BEHIND HAWNBY

The village of Hawnby sits above the River Rye in the upper reaches of the dale. Behind the village, the hills rise to join the moors of the Cleveland Hills but not before they produce two striking summits immediately behind the village itself. This walk takes the opportunity to climb both of these, Hawnby Hill and Easterside Hill, and explore the moors beyond. Here you will experience a rare opportunity on the North York Moors, a walk along a narrow ridge line with spectacular views in all directions.

DISTANCE: 7.2 miles / 11.5 km.
ASCENT: 1,250 feet / 381 metres.
TERRAIN: This walk encompasses a variety of terrain ranging from field and moorland paths to moorland tracks with even a little bit of heather bashing if you decide to explore the prehistoric field system that is encountered on the route. As the walk goes over the top of Hawnby Hill and almost to the top of Easterside Hill then there are two fairly steep climbs and correspondingly steep descents although they are not that particularly long. The other climbs on the route are a lot more gradual.
TIME: 4½ to 5 hours.
 START: Hawnby Village Hall car park GR SE 542 894. This is located in the lower half of the village just past the village shop and tea rooms. The car park itself is behind the village hall. Although there is no parking charge, people using the car park are asked to make a donation to village hall funds.
DOGS: At the time of test walking there were no signs prohibiting dogs and most of the route is on rights of way where they are allowed. However, as this is sheep grazing land please keep them under close control preferably on a lead. You may want to anyway as you go over Hawnby Hill, as there is a steep drop to either side.
ACCESS: The start of the walk, going over Hawnby Hill, is on access paths although most of the route after that is on public rights of way. There are parts of the route where the tracks do not strictly adhere to the rights of way but the route across the moor is all open access land and so does not create any problems.

GRID REFERENCES

Car park	542 894
Cairn	540 907
Moor Gate	540 917
Track junction	542 930

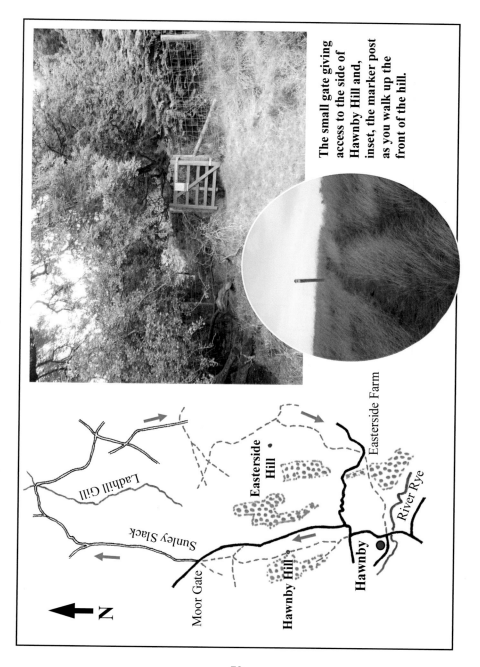

The small gate giving access to the side of Hawnby Hill and, inset, the marker post as you walk up the front of the hill.

Track junction	545 935
Bridge	550 936
Track crossroads	556 929
Row of stones	555 928
Track junction	554 926
Gate	557 919
Path/track junction	554 917
Path	554 915
Path junction/stile	557 907
Marker post	554 902
Path/road junction	553 897
Bridge	547 894
Car park	542 894

FGS GRADING

Grading is F6 [D1, N1, T1, R1, H2]

Distance	1	6 – 12 miles
Navigation	1	Basic navigation skills needed
Terrain	1	50 – 75% on graded track or path, 25 – 50% off track
Remoteness	1	Countryside in fairly close proximity to habitation – at least 80% of the route within 2 miles
Height	2	Over 125 ft per mile

THE WALK

1. Leave the car park and turn right to go past the tea rooms, back to the road junction. Here turn left to follow the road uphill to the upper part of the village and when you get to the top of the bank you'll come to another road junction, next to the Inn at Hawnby.

Continue straight ahead, crossing the junction, and go up the steps to the right of the bus shelter and then head up the lane between the houses. After a short distance you'll come to a gate with two waymarkers, a more prominent one pointing right and a faded one pointing left. Go through the gate and bear to the left towards a visible marker post a short way up the hillside. Ignore the waymarked stile to the left of the marker post and continue on, past the post, to the top corner of the field where you will find a small gate with an access sign on it.

Go through the gate and follow the path running next to the fence. The path soon bears away from the fence to head steeply uphill through the bracken, passing through a gate as it goes. Continue climbing and not long after passing an access waymarker post the climb starts to level out a bit. It's not long before you come to a large stone cairn. **GR 540 907.**

2. Continue on following the distinctive path as the hill top narrows to become a thin ridge line. The path runs along this ridge with Hawnby Hill Crag to the left and a steep descent down to the right. After a while you'll pass a ruined wall standing in a dip before coming to the high spot of the hill.

Following the ridge line of Hawnby Hill.

From here the road, track junctions and parking space at Moor Gate are clearly visible in front and below you. The path now starts to descend quite steeply down the back of the hill heading straight towards Moor Gate. After a steep descent the path comes to a rough track that cuts across your route while you are still on the shoulder of the hill, high above the road.

The path ends here but following the track in either direction would take you a fair distance away from Moor Gate. So bite the bullet and continue straight ahead over the track, going in a straight line over the moor making for Moor Gate. The walk across the heather is not too bad and the descent is a lot more gradual than the one just experienced. After a little while you'll join the road at a cattle grid. **GR 540 917.**

Heading towards Moor Gate.

3. Cross the cattle grid and head up the track that has the sign 'unsuitable for motor vehicles' at it's entrance. Follow the track as it slowly climbs up Sunley Slack heading towards the distant Bilsdale transmitter mast. After what seems a long steady climb, you'll come to a junction with a track that goes off to the right. **GR 542 930.**

4. Turn right here to follow the yellow surfaced track as it starts to head downhill into Ladhill Gill. After a little while you'll come to another track junction. **GR 545 935.**

5. Here turn right to continue heading downhill, passing some old workings by the side of the track. Within a short distance, the track passes a ruined building and then a marker post before coming to a gate. Pass through the gate and continue down to where the Ladhill Beck is joined by a side-stream and here a pipe bridge and shallow ford take you across both water courses. **GR 550 936.**

6. At this point a couple of paths and rough tracks meet the obvious main track but stay on the main track as it climbs up the other side of the shallow valley. At the top of the bank ignore the rough track that leaves the right side and stay on the main track as it bends to the left to go across the ridge line.

After 400/500metres the track approaches a gate and wall that line the other side of the ridge. Here, just in front of the gate, you'll come to a track crossroads. **GR 556 929.**

7. Don't go through the gate, instead turn right to follow the rougher track as it heads towards the distinctive outline of Easterside Hill. After 100/200 metres you'll pass a white-topped post on the left side of the track. Here, just a few metres in from the track (**GR 555 928**), lies a low row of stones that form the remains of a boundary wall from the prehistoric field system that lies across this ridge.

The row of stones are the remains of a Bronze Age/Iron Age field system that could date back over 3,000 years to a time of more favourable weather conditions, when these hilltop ridges were prime grazing and growing land. The system is comprised of a number of irregular shaped cultivation plots separated by collapsed stone walls, many of the walls since having their stones removed probably for the more modern intake walls of the surrounding fields. The field system was first surveyed in 1963 when, along with the walls, a large number of clearance cairns and a hut circle were found in an area that covered 700 metres x 400 metres. Unfortunately, most of these remains are now covered by thick heather and, apart from the large obvious traces, are difficult to see at first glance. The system is a scheduled ancient monument.

Return to the track and continue along it for another few hundred metres until you come to a junction where another rough track crosses the one that you are on. Conveniently a white-topped post on the left helps mark the junction. **GR 554 926.**

8. Here turn left to follow the new track towards the visible wall in the near distance. As you head towards the wall, the track passes through some of the stone walls that run along the surface of the moor.

When the track arrives at the wall it doesn't go through the gate in front but instead bends to the right to follow the wall, keeping it on your left. At this point the best example of the prehistoric walls can be seen on your right running in a line across the moor.

The prehistoric walls running across the moor.

78

Follow the track as it shadows the wall, going past another gate in the wall. After a while you'll come to a second gate, this one with a faded waymarker on it. It also lies just in front of a large pile of stones. **GR 557 919.**

9. At the gate turn right to follow a distinctive path that at first heads up a narrow gully before climbing up it's left side to become a narrow but followable path through the heather. The path twists and turns it's way through the heather to eventually join an eroded track. **GR 554 917.**

10. When you have joined the track, don't immediately follow it. Instead look over to the left towards the distinctive shape of Easterside Hill to see a wall a short distance away. Head over the heather towards the wall and just in front of it come to a path. **GR 554 915.**

11. Turn left to follow the path as it runs alongside the wall, keeping the wall on your right. The path is well-walked and easy to follow as it circles round the side of the hill, slowly descending as it goes and along the way passing a marker post. Eventually you'll come to a path junction with a waymarked stile on the right. **GR 557 907.**

Approaching the path junction and the stile in the wall.

12. Here turn right to leave the path and cross over the stile. Once on the other side follow the path which initially follows the side of a fence before leaving it to start climbing up over the shoulder of Easterside. Although not too steep, the climb does get the heart and legs pumping.

As you approach the top of the climb you'll pass a marker post and then as you come to the top of the shoulder you'll come to a second (**GR 554 902**). Here, at this second post, a faint path leads off on the right to travel the 500 metres or so to the summit of the hill. If you fancy an out and back diversion feel free to have a little walk to the summit.

Following the path over the shoulder of Easterside Hill.

If not, then continue on the path as it now starts to turn to the left and descend following a series of marker posts. In places the descent can be quite steep and during the height of summer, tall bracken can partially hide the path, so be careful where you place your feet. The descent gives good views out over Ryedale, with Hawnby not too far away over to the right.

Continue downhill to come to a stile which you cross into a field. Now follow the fence on the left, ignoring any stiles that cross it, and as you approach the bottom of the field bear right towards a stile to the right of the bottom gate which leads onto the roadside. **GR 553 897.**

13. Cross the road to the footpath marker on the opposite side and go through the gate into the field. The direction shown by the footpath marker is slightly out so don't blindly follow it. Instead head diagonally down across the field to the left of the first electricity pole, to come to the bottom fence of the field where you will find a gate and stile underneath the overhanging trees.

Cross the stile into the wood and then follow the path through the narrow belt of trees. Once past these, the path enters a small field and here turns to the left to go down to a gate. Go through the gate to enter a long open field and now follow the path as it heads down the length of the field.

Following the path down the field.

As you get towards the bottom of the field you'll have to cross the line of an obvious ditch, the bottom of which is a little soft and muddy. After this, turn right to the edge of the field to find a waymarked stile and footbridge hidden in the trees. **GR 547 894.** If you miss the ditch and continue down the field then you'll come to a fence and gate, in which case you'll know that you have come too far and you'll need to retrace your steps.

14. Cross the stile and footbridge and follow the path across the next field to a waymarked gate. Go through and the buildings of Hawnby can be seen directly in front, follow the path as it heads directly towards them to come to a gate that leads onto the road at the road junction in the lower half of the village. Cross the road and head up the side road, passing the Hawnby Stores and Tea Rooms, to come back to the village hall and it's car park.

**Exiting Roppa Plantation onto the open moor.
Close to here was the scene of a brutal murder
in the 1800's.
Walk 8: Roppa Edge and the Magna Via.**

WALK 8: ROPPA EDGE AND THE MAGNA VIA

Roppa Edge lies just over five miles away from Helmsley amongst the Forestry Commission's Newgate Bank plantation. However, don't look for the name Roppa Bank on the map, according to the OS it goes by a number of names such as Rievaulx Bank, Ayton Bank and Helmsley Bank but to the local population it is simply Roppa Bank. The name Roppa coming from Rauthe, meaning 'Red' and may refer to the presence of red shale or ironstone.

This is a walk that touches history but in many more ways than you would expect. Here the landscape is in direct contact with the past and you can see traces of our prehistoric ancestors, travel in the footsteps of William the Conqueror, see innovative ways of providing water to 18th century villages and experience the suffering during the Second World War. And on top of all that, you can brush close to the scene of a brutal 19th century murder.

DISTANCE: 8.4 miles / 13.5 km.
ASCENT: 876 feet / 267 metres.
START: The Forestry Commission car park at Newgate Bank on the B1257 Helmsley to Stokesley road, approximately five miles north of Helmsley. GR SE 564 889.
TIME: 4¾ to 5¼ hours.
TERRAIN: A mixture of moor and woodland paths and tracks. The outward path across the moor, following the route of the Magna Via, is nowadays a narrow walker's path and while distinctive and normally easy to follow, can in places be overgrown by tall heather and can also be wet and boggy. The climbing on this walk is mainly slow and gradual, however, the final sting in the tail is a long, steady climb up through the woods back to the car park.
ACCESS: The majority of the route is on public rights of way although most of the route coming back over the moor uses shooters tracks over access land.
DOGS: Although the majority of this route is on public rights of way, large chunks of the route are over access land and here, unfortunately, dogs are not allowed.

GRID REFERENCES

Car park	564 889
Rievaulx Moor	569 893
Track/road junction	594 903

83

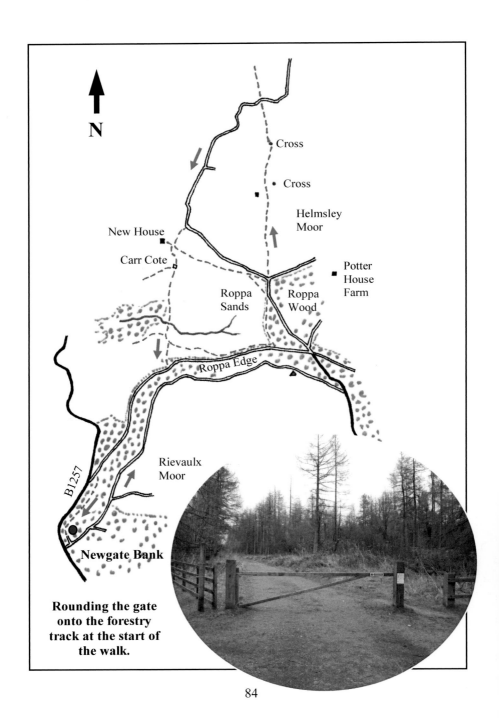

N

Cross

Cross

Helmsley
Moor

New House

Carr Cote

Potter
House
Farm

Roppa
Sands

Roppa
Wood

Roppa Edge

B1257

Rievaulx
Moor

Newgate Bank

**Rounding the gate
onto the forestry
track at the start of
the walk.**

Track crossroads	590 908
Gate and stile	586 916
Stream crossing	586 923
Roppa Cross South	587 926
Roppa Cross North	587 930
Path/track junction	586 935
Track corner	578 922
Stile	576 920
Stile	576 913
Old shaft	576 912
Stile	576 911
Gate and stile	576 909
Gate	577 908
Track/path junction	568 897
Car park	564 889

FGS GRADING

Grading is F5 [D1, N1, T1, R1, H1]

Distance	1	6 – 12 miles
Navigation	1	Basic navigation skills needed
Terrain	1	50 – 75% on graded track or path, 25 – 50% off track
Remoteness	1	Countryside in fairly close proximity to habitation – at least 80% of the route within 2 miles
Height	1	Over 100 ft per mile

THE WALK

1. From the main car park, return almost back to the road to come to a footpath marker post on the left and here, following the direction of the footpath arm, turn left and go round the gate onto the forestry track. The track is now followed through the trees, ignoring a junction with another track on the right, for 400/500 metres to emerge onto the open landscape of Rievaulx Moor. **GR 569 893.**

Following the track round the edge of the moor and, inset, the white-washed trig point.

2. Continue on the track as it follows the left-hand fence and ignore the track that goes off on the right just 50 metres after entering the moor. The track bends round the edge of the moor, slowly climbing all the time and passes two paths going downhill into the woods on the left. Here the landscape, with the slowly rising moor on the right and the sudden drop of Roppa Edge to the left, gives spectacular views in every direction. Eventually you'll pass the white-washed trig point on top of the moor and a short distance after that you'll come to the side of a narrow road. **GR 594 903.**

The road marks the route of the Magna Via which at this point is metaled and still used as a thoroughfare albeit only intermittently.

3. Turn left to follow the road downhill. As you walk down the bank, the Bilsdale transmitter mast rises in front of you, perfectly framed between the trees. Once at the bottom of the bank, the road ends at a crossroads of tracks with a marker post alongside. **GR 590 908.**

4. Ignore the tracks on either side and continue straight ahead to the junction that is just a few metres in front and here bear to the left, not the branch that goes down to Potter House.

Continue along the track and it soon starts to approach and run alongside the edge of the moor. At this point ignore the waymarked stile that goes over the

THE MAGNA VIA

The Magna Via, or Great Road, was an important Medieval road that ran north from Helmsley over the top of the moorland ridges to Stump Cross on Bilsdale Moor where it joined the Thurkilsti, another important Medieval road. At this time the majority of the routeways across the moors followed the ridgeways, the higher ground between the dales provided the firmer surface, avoiding bogs and rocky ground.

The road left Helmsley and followed, on what is now a tarmac lane, Baxton's Rigg, passing the various Baxton's farms, to Roppa Edge. After descending the Edge the route continued north across the moor, going over Bilsdale East Moor before arriving at Stump Cross.

The route was already well-established by the time that it was mentioned in the grant of land to Rievaulx Abbey by Walter Espec in 1145. Although a tarmac road until you reach the foot of Roppa Bank and from there a track through Roppa Woods, once you exit the woods the routeway is now no more than a thin path through the heather and once on the high moors is non-existent altogether.

In places a series of hollow ways shadow the path, pathways worn into the ground by centuries of heavy use. Local tradition has it that this roadway was used by William the Conqueror and his army to return to Helmsley during his 'Harrying of the North' campaign where he laid waste to the northern counties in order to subdue the rebellious lords..

The route of the Magna Via going down Roppa Edge and, inset, a series of parallel paths, or hollow ways, worn into the ground as the road crosses the moor.

fence onto the moor (**GR 586 914**) and continue along the track to come to a waymarked gate and stile that lead onto the open moor. **GR 586 916.**

Making for the small stone cairn after crossing the stile.

5. Cross the stile and turn right for 2/3 metres to a small stone cairn on the left side of the track that marks the start of a narrow path that goes off over the moor. Turn left to follow this path as it starts a gradual climb alongside a deep gully on the left.

The small stream that runs in the deeply carved gully next to the path is part of what once was Carlton Race. On the southern part of the North York Moors, many of the settlements were built on porous limestone and so there was little chance of a reliable water source for these villages and hamlets. During the 1700's a remarkable engineer named Joseph Foord hit on the idea of collecting water on the high moors and then using constructed channels called 'races' to funnel this water to the settlements. Some of these races ran for considerable distances, Carlton Race itself started on Bilsdale East Moor and ran for

The path is well-walked and fairly easy to follow although in places where the heather has grown quite tall, it may hide it. The path stays to the right of the gully but eventually, after about 700 metres, the sides of the gully become eroded and the path drops down to cross the shallow flow of water. **GR 586 923.**

6. Here don't follow the obvious path straight ahead which heads towards an unusual shape on the skyline but instead bear right to a small stone cairn which marks the correct path which now runs on the left of the gully. Continue along the path and after 200 metres you'll be level with the unusual shape which stands just over a 100 metres away on the left. This shape turns out to be a small, brick-built building.

The strangely shaped brick building dates back to the Second World War and served as a shelter/control building for RAF personnel who manned a practice bombing range which was sited on the moor over which you are walking. Only non-explosive practice bombs were used on the range and after the war these were cleared up, although pound to a penny there is still one or two hidden in the heather.

On the night of 16 May, 1944, Lancaster KB701 took off from RAF Goosepool, now Durham Tees Valley Airport, near Darlington for night bombing practice on the range. While flying low to avoid low fog, the aircraft flew into the moor over towards Potter House Farm. Sadly all seven crew were killed in the crash.

As you walk along the path, turn your eyes to the right and 100 metres after passing the shelter, you'll see the first of two medieval stone crosses that marked the Magna Via. The cross lies 100 metres to the right side of the path but it is easy enough to cross the gully when level with it and walk across for a closer look. **GR 587 926.**

Roppa Cross South.

Standing about 100 metres away from the path, Roppa Cross South is thought to have been originally erected as a waymarker on the Magna Via which may have run closer to the cross than the current path. The cross is one of two that stand along the route of this road as it passes over Roppa Moor.

What you see now is only part of the original cross. This would have stood approximately 2 metres high, about 6 foot 5 inches. The top of the cross is placed precariously on part of the shaft, another piece of stone which may be part of the original shaft lies next to it in the heather. Look closely at the cross top and you'll see that it is formed with a carved wheel head with a Maltese Cross just visible inside it.

---

7. Continue along the path, after another 400 metres you'll come to the second Roppa Moor cross. **GR 587 930.** This cross being right alongside the path although the remains are not quite as well preserved as the first.

Roppa Cross North.

The northern cross stands just a ¼ mile from it's sister. In all probability the two would have looked fairly similar when newly erected but now very little remains of this one, just a short length of broken shaft wedged into a stone base.

The path continues and in places what appears to be a sunken path/track appears on the right side of it. Possible evidence of a heavily used Magna Via in past times.

The path now starts a slow descent, going down the other side of the moorland hill and it's not long before a yellow dolomite track can be seen in the near distance. This is the ultimate destination but before long the path joins a rough quad track which is followed straight ahead for a fairly short distance to pass between some grouse butts and join the dolomite track. **GR 586 935.**

8. Turn left onto the dolomite track and follow it to the edge of the valley. Here, ignoring the rough track that goes straight ahead downhill, follow the obvious main track as it turns left and runs along above the side of the valley.

The track has now turned and is heading back towards the woods on Roppa Edge. After a while the track passes a second track which goes off on the left **(GR 581 930)**, which you ignore, before eventually heading down towards a wall in front. When it gets there, the track follows the left-side of the wall for a couple of hundred metres before coming to a corner where it turns sharply left away from the wall. **GR 578 922.**

9. Here, on the bend, leave the track to follow a path that goes along the side of the wall as it goes through an area of large boulders. It's not long before the path comes to a waymarked stile over the wall. **GR 576 920.**

As you leave the track the path goes through an area of large boulders. Look amongst them and you will see what may be the remains of prehistoric field boundaries linking some of the stones. In appearance the walls look very similar to those encountered in Walks 4 and 7. However, no archaeological work has yet been undertaken here to determine their antiquity although a suspected prehistoric settlement is thought to exist a short distance away, on the side of the hill and if so, then the two would probably be connected.

10. Cross the stile and follow the right-hand wall for 40 metres or so to come to the top of a walled lane above the ruins of New House. Don't go down the lane but instead turn left to follow the wall, keeping it on your right. Go past the gap in the wall and stay with the wall as it bends to the left and goes past a large pile of stones, to come to a gate in front of the ruins of Carr Cote.

Go through the gate and head to the right-side of the ruins to the end of the partially ruined wall. Once at the end of the wall, go straight ahead, crossing an old track, and head downhill across the middle of the field. Halfway down the field you'll pass through a gateway in a wire fence and once through, continue downhill but bear to the bottom left-hand corner of the field where you will find a stile to cross the stone wall.

Cross the stile and go straight ahead with the line of trees on your left to come to another stile, this one just inside the trees, next to the stream. **GR 576 913.**

11. Cross and follow the right bank of the stream for about 20 metres to come to a marker post that shows the point where you cross. Cross the stream and follow the path up the bank on the other side to another marker post.

After reaching the top of the bank, the path now starts to descend, passing an old mine shaft on the way, **GR 576 912.**

The old shaft dates back several centuries and is a product of coal mining. There were a number of small scale pits operating here during the 1700/1800's providing a poor quality coal for both domestic use and to supply the local iron foundries in the neighbouring dales.

The path arrives at the edge of the valley of the Todhill Beck and then descends quite steeply down to the side of the water. Here take care while you descend as the path crosses some moss covered boulders which can be quite slippery.

Cross the beck, which is easier than it first looks, and go past another old shaft to a waymarked stile a short distance up the bank. **GR 576 911.**

12. Cross the stile and, following the direction of the waymarker on it, go up the bank to pass to the left of a couple of ruined buildings. Once past the ruins, a ladder stile becomes visible at the top of the field next to a faded white gate. **GR 576 909.**

Clamber over the stile to exit the field onto the moor and from here continue ahead but bearing slightly to the left to follow a green gully up the hill to the side of the wood. When you have climbed up to the wood's boundary fence, turn left to follow the fence, keeping it on your right, for a short distance to come to a small gate that leads into the wood. **GR 577 908.**

13. Pass through the gate and go straight ahead for a few metres to join a forest track. Here turn right to follow it. After a short distance, the trees on the right give way to open fields and then after 400/500 metres the track begins a steady descent.

Not long after, the fields end and the track is once again enclosed by trees on both sides and now the track begins to descend a bit more steeply. Eventually a road becomes visible a little distance in front and it's usually quite helpful if a car goes conveniently past at the same time. However, before you get to the road, you come to a bridleway marker post that points up a path on the left-hand side that goes quite steeply up the side of the hill. **GR 568 897.**

14. Leave the track to turn left and follow the path up the steep climb through the trees. A stiff climb now follows for about 300 metres before it eases off and the path continues round the side of the hill.

There are a couple of minor paths that branch off on the left but continue straight ahead and after about 500 metres, you'll pass underneath the observation platform on the left and then enter the car park where you can pull off your boots and relax.

MURDER MOST FOUL

On the morning of Sunday, July 16th, 1895, the bodies of a woman and her one-year old child were recovered from a shallow grave on the moor, close to where the path exits Roppa Plantation. The bodies were recovered by a small group of men led by a Mr Tyerman, who the previous Thursday had noticed the prepared grave while out mending roads. At the time he had assumed that it would be for a farmer burying a dead sheep but once he was back at Helmsley and heard the rumours of a missing woman and the suspected murder, he made the connection between the two.

The bodies in the grave were that of a Mrs Hudson and her baby, recently moved into Helmsley with her husband Robert Hudson. He had been brought up on these moors but after serving an apprenticeship as a cabinet maker in Darlington, had been working in the furniture industry in Nottingham. After losing his job there it appears that he brought his wife and child to see the country.

There is no doubt that the crime was premeditated, the grave had already been prepared and a carving knife hidden at the spot when he took his wife for a walk over the moors. When she was brought to the spot, Mrs Hudson must have struggled for the life of herself and her baby as her dress was cut and ripped and she had defensive wounds over her hands and arms. However, despite her struggles Hudson overpowered her and the carving knife was used to cut both his wife's and his baby's throats.

After returning to Helmsley, Hudson told conflicting tales about his wife going to see friends and also about her running off with another man before he himself departed for York. However, it wasn't long before rumours started to circulate about the disappearance of Mrs Hudson and then with the discovery of the bodies the search for her husband started. Eventually arrested and returned to Helmsley, Hudson was committed by the magistrates to the assizes at York. Here he was tried, condemned and eventually hanged in York Castle.

Where the tracks leave the plantation and the bodies of the unfortunate Mrs Hudson and her baby were found.

The prehistoric Cross Dyke.
Walk 9: Sunny Bank and Arden Hall.

WALK 9: SUNNY BANK AND ARDEN HALL

As we have seen in the two previous walks that go across the open moor, The Hills Behind Hawnby and The Rye Head Circular, there is ample evidence of prehistoric man and his settlements on these southern hills of the North York Moors. This walk explores the deeply cut valleys to the south-west of the River Rye and along the way discovers prehistoric monuments of a different kind, dykes and burial grounds.

DISTANCE: 6.4 miles / 10.2 km.
ASCENT: 1,093 feet / 333 metres.
TERRAIN: Mainly field and woodland paths and tracks. In both winter and wet weather some of these woodland paths can be quite muddy. Most of the climbing is fairly steady although there is a short but quite steep climb up from the footbridge across the River Rye towards the end of the walk.
TIME: 4 to 4½ hours.
START: Hawnby village hall car park. GR SE 542 894.
DOGS: As the route is on public rights of way, then dogs are allowed. However, please keep them under close control as livestock will be encountered at various points along the route.
ACCESS: The route is all on public rights of way. If you wish to explore the Cross Dyke and the burial mounds then there is a permissive access agreement in place that does allow you to do so.

GRID REFERENCES

Hawnby village hall	542 894
Path/track junction	542 892
Path/track junction	535 892
Gate	528 894
Track junction	513 895
Gate	511 902
Track junction	511 905
Track junction	519 905
Track junction	519 909
Path/track junction	525 910
Track/path junction	529 912
Footbridge	531 907
Footbridge	532 909
Path junction	534 910

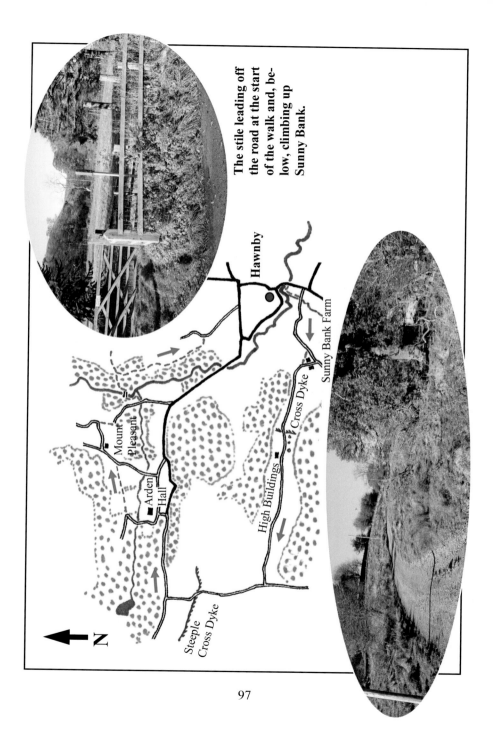

The stile leading off the road at the start of the walk and, below, climbing up Sunny Bank.

N

Hawnby

Sunny Bank Farm

Cross Dyke

High Buildings

Mount Pleasant

Arden Hall

Steeple Cross Dyke

Track/road junction	541 898
Hawnby village hall	542 894

FGS GRADING

Grading is T6 [D1, N1, T1, R1, H2]

Distance	1	6 – 12 miles
Navigation	1	Basic navigation skills needed
Terrain	1	50 – 75% on graded track or path, 25 – 50% off track
Remoteness	1	Countryside in fairly close proximity to habitation – at least 80% of the route within 2 miles
Height	2	Over 125 ft per mile

THE WALK

1. Exit the car park and turn right to head past the tea rooms back to the main road. Once there, turn right to cross the River Rye by the Hawnby Bridge. When you are on the other side of the bridge, you'll come to a footpath marker post on the right-side of the road next to a gate and a smaller pedestrian gate. As the small sign says, the footpath here has been diverted and so doesn't quite match up with the map. Leave the road to go through the small pedestrian gate and follow the path as it runs next to the river.

After a 100 metres or so, the path comes to a junction where a small stream enters the Rye and here bears left to follow the stream and comes to a small gate. Go through and continue on the path, with a fence on your left, to come to a stile leading onto a track. **GR 542 892.**

2. Cross the stile and turn right to follow the track across a cattle grid that goes over the stream. The track now starts climbing up the side of the hill. After a while the track goes through a gateway, crossing a cattle grid, and then bears to the left.

Stay on the track for another 200 metres until you come to the point where there is a wooden gate on the right-hand side. The gate is not marked but there is a

Approaching the gate on the right of the track and, inset, looking up from the gate.

marker post stood next to it although there are no direction arms to the post. Leave the track to turn right through this gate and follow the right-hand hedge up across the field to a second gate, this one being waymarked.

Go through the gate and, following the blue bridleway marker, go straight ahead up the bank to join a track next to a marker post, with Sunnybank Farm lying just to your left. **GR 535 892.**

3. Turn right onto the track following the direction for Dale Town Common and go past the track on the left next to a second marker post that you ignore. Stay on the track as it curves round and up the hill to come to a waymarked gateway.

Go through and continue on the track. After a short distance the track forks but here it doesn't matter which branch you take as they both end up in the same place, meeting up in front of a waymarked double-gate. **GR 528 894.**

The gate is set within a stone wall which stands on the Cross Dyke, a prehistoric earthwork running across the ridge of Sunny Bank.

4. Go through the gate and continue on the track, passing the prehistoric graveyard on the left and an old quarry and lime kiln on the right, to pass the barns of High Buildings. Pass through the gateway after the barns and continue follow-

SUNNY BANK

As you approach the gate, it is easy to see that the wall in which it is set seems to be higher than you would expect. The wall itself has been built upon the top of a bank 0.5 metres high, continuing a practice that began three thousand years ago between the Bronze and Iron Ages. Once through the gate you'll see that on the other side, a substantial ditch 5 metres wide and 1 metre deep runs the length of the wall.

The northern side of the Cross Dyke and, inset, inside the southern side of the Dyke.

This is the Cross Dyke, a ditch with a bank on either side which runs 180 metres across the spur of land between Gower Dale to the south and the valley of the Dalicar Beck to the north. The Dyke is part of a wider system of prehistoric earthworks that stretch across the western side of the Hambleton Hills. Built at some point between the Bronze Age and the Iron Age, the Dyke enhanced the natural division of the land by river valleys and watersheds and formed a territorial boundary dividing the land into units. At the time pastoralism, especially cattle ranching, was a predominant form of agriculture. The impressive scale of this and the other earthworks on these hills also displayed the power and wealth of their builders.

Located just a little bit further in from the Dyke lies what is a prehistoric round barrow cemetery. The cemetery dates back to the Bronze Age, around 2,000 to

700 BC, and will have been used for a considerable time period, typically over a period of centuries. These barrows stand out as low circular earth and stone mounds around 6 metres in diameter. In total there are nine mounds each holding either a single or multiple burial although in other similar sites further burials have often been found in the ground between the mounds.

One of the burial mounds and, inset, the hollow top of one of the mounds showing where it has been disturbed .

One unusual feature about this cemetery is that it was re-used during the early medieval period. Excavations during the 19th century showed that the tombs had been opened up and later, Anglo-Saxon burials had been inserted into the mounds. One discovery was that of a young Anglo-Saxon woman with gold and silver hair pins, a stone spindle whorl and a bronze bowl.

Each of the mounds was surrounded by a ditch up to 3 metres wide although over time these have since become filled-in and are no longer visible to the eye. Most of the mounds have been disturbed in the past probably through 19th century excavations and treasure hunters and now sport a hollow top.

As you head towards the barns, on the right-side of the track you'll also pass a shallow quarry. Built into the side of it are the remains of an old lime kiln, the obvious recipient of the stone produced from the quarry. The limestone was burnt to produce an early fertiliser used to 'sweeten' the grass and produce the grazing fields on top of these hills.

ing the track, with the fence on your right, heading towards the distant trees.

After a little while the track passes through a second gateway before coming to another gate that leads onto the open moor. Go through this and continue straight ahead for about 20 metres to come to the side of a grass track. **GR 513 895.**

5. Turn right to follow the grass track, going past the brick structure and small quarry on the right next to the fence. As you progress along the track a couple of minor tracks come in from the left but stay on the obvious main track as it runs alongside the fence which shortly becomes a wall.

As the track draws level with the corner that marks the end of the wall, it turns to the left and descends into a dip to come to a gate. **GR 511 902.**

Descending the dip to the gate.

The dip is the top of Stoney Gill Hole, a natural feature that was used as part of Steeple Cross Dyke.

STEEPLE CROSS DYKE

Similar to the previously encountered Cross Dyke, the Steeple Cross Dyke is a prehistoric linear boundary system that still exists in the form of a very prominent earthwork. This dyke is part of what is known as the Cleave Dyke system, a series of linear ditches and banks that run north to south for over 9 km along the western escarpment of the Hambleton Hills. This section starting from here, the head of Stony Gill Hole, runs for 1,550 metres to the western face of the Hambleton Hills where it would have meet the line of another dyke in the system.

The name Steeple Cross comes from a medieval cross located towards the western end of the Dyke. Sadly only a small part of the cross, a short section of cross shaft, remains standing in the ground.

The eastern side of Steeple Cross Dyke and, inset, the western side.

6. Go through the gate and continue on the track as it climbs up the other side and then, at the top, bears slightly right to go across the top of the ridge heading towards the trees of Thorodale. As you cross the flat top of the ridge, the track starts to descend to join a vehicle track next to the woods. **GR 511 905.**

7. Turn right to follow the track downhill, passing the quarries of Arden Bank as you go.

Surprisingly enough this track is the road to Kepwick that is signposted in the centre of Hawnby.

After you have passed the quarries, pass through a gate to enter the woods. Continue on the track passing another track, on the left, as you descend. When you come to the bottom of the bank you'll come to a junction of tracks with the track going straight ahead continuing as a tarmac road, a road sign and the entrance to Arden Hall on the left. **GR 519 905.**

The entrance to Arden Hall.

8. Here turn left, following the direction of the bridleway sign, and go through the entrance to the hall. Follow the drive as it heads towards the Hall and then turns left going past a vehicle no entry sign. The drive passes to the left of the cottages before turning right to pass round the back of them, going between the cottages on the right and the outbuildings on the left.

At the end of the buildings continue straight ahead on a track heading downhill following the bridleway sign. The track goes down to cross a bridge over a stream before bending to the right and climbing up the other side of the valley.

At the top of the bank you'll come to a track junction with a gate on the right leading into an open field. **GR 519 909.**

9. Here turn right to go through the gate and enter the field, following the rough track with the fence on your right. After a short distance the track turns right to go through a gate and here leave it to continue going straight ahead, still with the fence on your right.

Stay to the left of the fence, ignoring any stiles that go into the woods that are now on your right and pass through a wide gap in a line of trees. Continue following the fence to come to a waymarked gate leading onto a farm track. **GR 525 910.**

10. Turn left onto the track and head towards the farm of Mount Pleasant. As you approach the farm, go through and over the gateway and cattle grid to come to a junction and here turn right to follow the track between the buildings to come to another gateway.

Go through and follow the track as it heads downhill back into the Rye valley. When you get to the bend where the track turns sharply left, you'll find a gate and a waymarked stile on the right side of the track. **GR 529 912.**

Descending into the Rye valley and, inset, the stile at the track bend.

11. Here turn right to leave the track and cross the stile into the field. Follow the left-hand fence across the field to come to a waymarked gate leading into the woods.

Enter and follow the track that you'll find on the other side of the gate as it continues the descent into the valley. After a short distance you'll pass another track on the right but continue heading downhill to come to the valley floor and a footbridge crossing a stream. **GR 531 907.**

12. Cross the bridge and immediately turn left through a waymarked gate and go to the second bridge that re-crosses the stream. Once on the other side of this bridge, follow the waymarker and go straight ahead to a marker post which, in turn, directs you left to a waymarked gate.

You are now at the side of the River Rye albeit on the top of a high bank. Ahead of you, further upstream, can be seen the curved arch of a substantial footbridge over the river. Go through the gate and follow the path upstream to come to the bridge. **GR 532 909.**

13. Cross the bridge and once on the other side follow the path as it bears left and then right, to start climbing up the other side of the valley. At the top of the bank you'll come to a waymarked gate on your left that leads into a field and a path that goes further into the woods on your right. **GR 534 910.**

The footbridge over the Rye.

14. Ignore the gate on the left and turn right to follow the path between the trees. The path is distinguishable and easy to follow although at one point it does appear to split but very quickly re-joins again.

The path eventually comes to the end of the woods and arrives at a waymarked gate that leads into a field. Go through and initially start following the track but then bear left to go up the slope of the hill to the gateway next to Carr House.

Go through and pick up a track on the other side which you then follow down and across the field until the point where it turns sharply right. Here leave the track to continue straight ahead to a waymarked gate.

Pass through the gate and follow the grass track as it goes straight ahead to the corner of the trees in front and then follows the left-side of the trees. After a few hundred metres you'll start to hear the thump, thump noise of the pump at Broach Well which you pass to the right of. Not long after this, the trees on the right end and you come to a gate. Pass through to join a track which you then follow straight ahead, passing through two fields, before coming to the roadside opposite Manor Farm. **GR 541 898.**

15. Turn left to follow the road the very short distance into Hawnby and when you get to the junction next to the pub, turn right to follow the road downhill into the lower section of the village. At the bottom of the bank turn right to go past the tea rooms and arrive at the village hall car park.

APPENDIX

Ferguson Grading System (`FGS`)

1. Introduction

The FGS has been adopted as a means of assessing the nature and severity of the various walks in this book and the abilities and equipment needed to tackle each one safely. The FGS was developed by Stuart Ferguson, a long time fell and trail runner, climber, mountaineer, mountain-biker and general outdoor enthusiast. In the opinion of Trailguides, the FGS is the most accurate and comprehensive grading system for comparing off-road walking, running and mountain-biking routes anywhere in the country.

2. The System

Tables 1 & 2, set out below, are used in order to give a grading to each route. Table 1 sets out three categories of country that a route could potentially cross, together with a range of factors that would need to be considered when tackling that route. The three categories are, Trail, Fell and Mountain, and after assessing which category best fits the route, a letter, either `T`, `F` or `M`, is allocated to that route. Where a route does not fit perfectly into one of the three categories the closest category is allocated.

Table 2 deals with five specific aspects of the route namely distance, navigation, terrain, remoteness and height gain, and each one is allocated a letter, `D`, `N`, `T`, `R`, and `H`. Each letter is also given a severity score from the range 0-3 or 0-4, in respect of distance (`D`). The higher the number, the more severe the route. The five severity scores are then added together to give an overall score. The overall score is then put with the Table 1 category letter (i.e. `T`, `F` or `M`).

In order to show how the grading has been determined for each walk in this book, the five individual severity scores are set out, in square brackets, immediately after the actual grading. So, for example, Walk 9 Sunny Bank and Arden Hall has a grading of T6 [D1, N1, T1, R1, H2], indicating that it is a Trail Category walk with a total severity score of 6. This is made up of the five specific severity scores, for distance (`D`), navigation (`N`), terrain (`T`), remoteness (`R`) and height gain (`H`), of 1, 1, 1, 1 and 2 respectively. The highest total severity score which can be achieved is 16 and the lowest total severity score achievable is 0.

The table which accompanies the grading at the start of each walk sets out the specific factors, extracted from Table 2, that need to be considered when tackling that particular walk.

TABLE 1

	TRAIL	FELL	MOUNTAIN
Description	Lowland and forest areas including urban, cultivated and forested locations.	Moorlands and upland areas which may include some upland cultivated and forestry areas plus possibly remote locations.	Upland and mountain areas including remote and isolated locations.
Height	Not usually above 1,000 feet but may go up to 2,500 feet	Usually above 1,000 feet, up to 2,500 feet and above.	Usually above 2,500 feet and up to 4,000 feet.
Way-marking	Usually	Limited	None
Terrain	Usually graded paths, tracks and trails but may include some off-trail	May include some graded paths, tracks and trails but mainly off-trail	Virtually all off-trail
Height gain	Limited height gain	May include considerable height gain	May include some severe height gain.
Effects of weather	Very limited effect	May be prone to sudden weather changes	Extreme weather a possibility
Navigational skills	None to basic	Basic to competent	Competent to expert
Equipment	Walking shoes/boots. Possibly waterproofs Food and drink dependant upon route.	3/4 season walking boots. Possibly map and compass dependant upon route. Food and drink dependant upon route.	Mountain boots. Full waterproof cover. Map and compass. Food and drink
Escape Routes	Yes	Some	Some to nil

TABLE 2

Score	0	1	2	3	4
Distance	Up to 6 miles	6 – 12 miles	12 – 18 miles	18 miles +	24 miles +
Navigation	No navigation skills needed	Basic navigation skills needed	Competent navigation skills needed	Expert navigation skills needed	
Terrain	75% + on graded track or path	50 – 75% on graded track or path 25 – 50% off track	25 -50% on graded track or path 50 – 75% off track	Under 25% on graded track or path Over 75% off track	
Remoteness	Urban	Countryside in fairly close proximity to habitation – at least 80% of the route within 2 miles	Countryside not in close proximity to habitation – less than 20% of the route within 2 miles	Remote, isolated location	
Height gain	Less than 100 ft per mile	Over 100 ft per mile	Over 125 ft per mile	Over 250 ft per mile	

Notes to Table 1

Graded paths = Well established paths with a stable surface.

Escape routes = The opportunity to cut the route short and return to the start without completing the full course in the event of weather changes or unforeseen incidents.

The Author

Keven Shevels

Kev has been involved with outdoor sports since his school days when participation in the Duke of Edinburgh award revealed the beauties of hill and dale and resulted in him walking or running through the countryside of the North East and beyond for most of the last forty years. Many of these trips into the great outdoors being visits to the heather-clad uplands of the North York Moors, an area for which he has developed a great fondness.

Over the last six years, Kev has put pen to paper describing routes through the North Pennines that reveal his passion for both the countryside and the history that has shaped it and the people who live upon it. That, coupled with an in-built curiosity to go and view things that spark his interest, tend to result in routes that take the reader into new, undiscovered areas and reveal a history that may not be apparent from the outside. He is not ashamed to admit that he is one of these boring people who can sit and spend hours reading a map like more normal people read a book. His great delight is coming up with new routes that he can subsequently explore and investigate. All of this has resulted in an easy to read, informative style of guidebook that has proved very popular among the walking fraternity and received very favourable reviews in both local and national press.

Now Kev returns to one of his favourite areas, the North York Moors, and in this, the second in a number of books that he is planning on the Moors, he explores the area around Helmsley following the valley of the River Rye up into the Moors themselves.

The author having a break out in the Durham countryside.

110

Walking North East

Walking North East is the brand name for the walking publications produced by Trailguides and reflects the pride that we, as North Easterners, have in our countryside, our history and our culture. Based in Darlington, we are a small independent publisher specialising in guidebooks centred on the North Eastern counties of England. Our target is to produce guides that are as user-friendly, easy to use and provide as much information as possible and all in an easily readable format. In essence, to increase the enjoyment of the user and to showcase the very best of the great North Eastern countryside. Our series of books explores the heritage of us all and lets you see your region with new eyes, these books are written to not just take you on a walk but to investigate, explore and understand the objects, places and history that has shaped not just the countryside but also the people of this corner of England.

If you've enjoyed following the routes in this guide and want news and details of other publications that are being developed under the Walking North East label then look at the company website at **www.trailguides.co.uk**

Comments and, yes, criticisms, are always welcomed especially if you discover a change to a route. Contact us by email through the website or by post at Trailguides Limited, 35 Carmel Road South, Darlington, Co Durham DL3 8DQ.

Other walking books from Walking North East.
At the time of publication the following books are also available but with new titles being regularly added to our publication list keep checking our website. All of these publications can be purchased as books or downloads from our website.

County Durham.
Hamsterley Forest.
The Barningham Trail.
Ancient Stones.
Walks from Stanhope.
Mid-Teesdale Walks.
Walking in Weardale.
Walking in Teesdale.

Northumberland.
The Cheviot Hills.
Walks from Wooler.
The Hills of Upper Coquetdale.
Walks from Kirknewton.
Walks on the Wild Side: The Cheviot Hills.
Walks Around Rothbury and Coquetdale.
Walks in Hadrian's Wall Country

North Yorkshire.
Walking the Hills of Upper Swaledale.
Walks Around Gunnerside.
Walks around Reeth and Upper Swaledale.
Walking around Osmotherley and the Cleveland Hills.
Walking around Helmsley and Ryedale.

Have a look at our Facebook page - **Walking North East** for current news on ourselves and our publications. The page also contains news, views and articles on all aspects of walking within the North Eastern counties of Durham, Northumberland and North Yorkshire. Definitely well worth a look and clicking the Like button.

For those that don't have or want to use Facebook then why not subscribe to our monthly newsletter. Titled 'Walking North East' this contains the same news, views and articles as our Facebook page. Subscriptions are free with no obligation to purchase and can be made via our website at www.trailguides.co.uk . Previous issues of Walking North East can also be accessed free via the website.

Acknowledgements.

As always acknowledgements must be paid to my walking companion, Harry Manuel, who not only provides good company on the walk but also checks and proof reads my route descriptions as well as appearing as the 'model' on the occasional photo. The preparation of this book would be a lot harder without him. I've also got to thank Lyn, my wife, for having the patience to allow me to disappear on these little expeditions.

Disclaimer

The information contained in these pages and the route descriptions is provided in good faith, but no warranty is made for its accuracy. The contents are, at the time of writing and to the best of our knowledge, up-to-date and correct. However, the world is a changing environment and what is correct one day may not be so the next. Care should always be taken when following these route descriptions just as it should when following maps or waymarkers of any kind..

No guarantee whatsoever is provided by the author and/or Trailguides Limited and no liability is accepted for any loss, damage or injury of any kind resulting from the use of this book, nor as a result of any defect or inaccuracy in it.

As with all outdoor activities, you and you alone are responsible for your safety and well being.